AIMR Conference Proceedings
Ethical Issues for Today's Firm

Proceedings of the AIMR seminar "In the Best Interests of Our Clients"

December 7–8, 1999
Philadelphia, Pennsylvania

Theodore R. Aronson, CFA, *moderator*
Charles B. Burkhart, Jr.
Thomas J. Dillman, CFA
Marianne M. Jennings
Kathryn B. McGrath

Andrew E. Nolan
Bluford H. Putnam
Wayne H. Wagner
James W. Ware, CFA
Jason Zweig

Association for Investment Management and Research

Dedicated to the Highest Standards of Ethics, Education, and Professional Practice in Investment Management and Research.

To obtain the *AIMR Publications Catalog,* contact:
AIMR, 560 Ray C. Hunt Drive, Charlottesville, Virginia 22903, U.S.A.
Phone 804-951-5499; Fax 804-951-5262; E-mail info@aimr.org
or
visit AIMR's World Wide Web site at www.aimr.org
to view the AIMR publications list.

CFA®, CHARTERED FINANCIAL ANALYST™, AIMR-PPS™, GIPS™, and Financial Analysts Journal® are just a few of the trademarks owned by the Association for Investment Management and Research. To view a list of the Association for Investment Management and Research's trademarks and the Guide for Use of AIMR's Marks, please visit our Web site at www.aimr.org.

©2000, Association for Investment Management and Research

All rights reserved. No part of this publication may be reproduced, stored in a retrieval system, or transmitted, in any form or by any means, electronic, mechanical, photocopying, recording, or otherwise, without prior written permission of the copyright holder.

AIMR Conference Proceedings (ISSN 1086-5055; USPS 013-739) is published four times a year in June, August, August, and December by the Association for Investment Management and Research, 560 Ray C. Hunt Drive, Charlottesville, Virginia 22903, U.S.A. This publication is designed to provide accurate and authoritative information with regard to the subject matter covered. It is sold with the understanding that the publisher is not engaged in rendering legal, accounting, or other professional services. If legal advice or other expert assistance is required, the services of a competent professional should be sought. Periodicals postage paid at the post office in Richmond, Virginia, and additional mailing offices.

Copies are mailed as a benefit of membership to CFA® charterholders. Subscriptions also are available at US$100 for one year. Address all circulation communications to AIMR Conference Proceedings, 560 Ray C. Hunt Drive, Charlottesville, Virginia 22903, U.S.A.; Phone 804-951-5499; Fax 804-951-5262. For change of address, send mailing label and new address six weeks in advance.

Postmaster: Send address changes to the Association for Investment Management and Research, P.O. Box 3668, Charlottesville, Virginia 22903.

ISBN 0-935015-50-7
Printed in the United States of America
July 2000

Editorial Staff

Katrina F. Sherrerd, CFA
Book Editor

Maryann Dupes
Editor

Christine E. Kemper
Assistant Editor

Cheryl L. Likness
Production Coordinator

Jaynee M. Dudley
Production Manager

Lois A. Carrier
Composition

Contents

Foreword . . . . Katrina F. Sherrerd, CFA	iv
Biographies	v
Overview: Ethical Issues for Today's Firm	1
Professional Responsibilities, Ethics, and the Law . . . . Marianne M. Jennings	4
You Get the Clients You Deserve . . . . Jason Zweig	13
Drawing the Line in a Gray Area . . . . James W. Ware, CFA	24
Corporate Conduct and Professional Integrity: A Survey . . . . Andrew E. Nolan	31
Measuring, Controlling, and Allocating Trading Costs . . . . Wayne H. Wagner	35
Attracting, Motivating, and Retaining Professionals . . . . Thomas J. Dillman, CFA	43
Managing Firm Risk . . . . Bluford H. Putnam	51
Competitive Challenges in the Investment Management Industry . . . . Charles B. Burkhart, Jr.	62
Selected Publications	70

Foreword

People tend to think of shady and unscrupulous characters as the ones who get something for nothing, and many people believe that investors get something (a lot of money) for a perceived nothing (no work); they simply put down some cash and wait for the big returns. Investing does not seem to require any blood, sweat, or tears. Although that perception is far from reality, it may help to explain why the ethics of the industry has always been suspect and why the investment management industry is often considered to be a playground for unethical people.

No one, and no industry, is perfect. The investment management industry has had unscrupulous characters who have acted in ways that no one would consider ethical. The industry, however, has also had people whose ethics are beyond reproach, but such individuals rarely make the news. It should come as no surprise that the ethics of those involved in the investment management industry range from the highly ethical to the highly unethical. Unfortunately, one typical solution to even out the wide range of ethical behavior is regulation and legislation. Why else would the U.S. Securities Exchange Act of 1934 stipulate that members of an exchange cannot manipulate prices of securities listed on the exchange? Apparently, Congress did not believe that it could rely on individuals to act ethically regarding price manipulation.

The authors in this proceedings are attempting to get people to focus on ethics because doing so is the right thing to do. Regulating and legislating ethical behavior should be the option of last resort. Furthermore, the authors clearly make the argument that good ethics is good business. And as these authors point out, discussing ethics in the investment management industry does not mean discussing simply the ethics of interacting with clients but also the ethics of interacting with fellow professionals as peers and coworkers and in supervisor/supervisee relationships. Ultimately, the continued success of the industry relies on how the industry addresses the issue of ethics.

We are especially grateful to Theodore R. Aronson, CFA, of Aronson+Partners for his efforts as moderator of this seminar. We also extend our sincere thanks to all the authors for their contributions to this book: Charles B. Burkhart, Jr., Investment Counseling, Inc.; Thomas J. Dillman, CFA, Scudder Kemper Investments; Marianne M. Jennings, Arizona State University; Andrew E. Nolan, PricewaterhouseCoopers LLP; Bluford H. Putnam, Bayesian Edge Technology & Solutions, Ltd.; Wayne H. Wagner, Plexus Group; James W. Ware, CFA, Winning with Style, Inc.; and Jason Zweig, *Money* magazine.

The idea that "nice guys finish last" is a pervasive one, and the converse of the saying would be "bad guys finish first." The authors in this proceedings challenge investment professionals to create their own saying: "nice (and ethical) guys finish first."

Katrina F. Sherrerd, CFA
Senior Vice President
Educational Products

Biographies

Theodore R. Aronson, CFA, is the managing partner of Aronson+Partners, which manages funds for institutional investors. Previously, he was a member of the Quantitative Equities Group at Drexel Burnham Lambert, where he provided innovative practical applications of modern portfolio theory and quantitative portfolio management. Mr. Aronson is a frequent speaker on Wall Street issues, especially on innovations in trading methods to minimize transaction costs. He serves as a regent of AIMR's Financial Analysts Seminar and as chair of programs for AIMR's Annual Conference. Mr. Aronson holds an M.B.A. from The Wharton School of the University of Pennsylvania.

Charles B. Burkhart, Jr., is founder and president of Investment Counseling, Inc. He also oversees the firm's mergers and acquisitions practice, broad strategy projects, and certain client relationships. He developed "Measuring Operating Efficiency" in 1990, one of the earliest studies of money management businesses and the forerunner to "Competitive Challenges." Prior to establishing Investment Counseling, Mr. Burkhart was a principal with the executive search firm of Lee Calhoon & Company, where he specialized in the field of pensions and investments. Mr. Burkhart is a frequent speaker and writer on trends and challenges in the investment management business. He holds a B.A. in English from Boston College.

Thomas J. Dillman, CFA, is Director of U.S. Research at Scudder Kemper Investments. Mr. Dillman formerly served as a senior vice president and director of research at State Street Research & Management Company, where he managed the Galileo Fund. Previously, he was the director of research at the Bank of New York. Mr. Dillman earned a B.A. and an M.Ed. at Lehigh University and an M.B.A. from The Wharton School of the University of Pennsylvania.

Marianne M. Jennings is professor of legal and ethical studies at Arizona State University. She served as director of the Joan and David Lincoln Center for Applied Ethics from 1995–1999. She has worked with the Federal Public Defender and U.S. Attorney in Nevada and has consulted for law firms, businesses, and professional groups. Professor Jennings has authored six textbooks and monographs and more than 130 articles. She is a contributing editor for the *Real Estate Law Journal* and *Corporate Finance Review*, writes a biweekly, nationally syndicated column for the *Arizona Republic*, and is a commentator on business issues on "All Things Considered" for National Public Radio. Professor Jennings holds an undergraduate degree and a J.D. from Brigham Young University.

Andrew E. Nolan is the managing partner of the Regulatory Compliance Consulting Group at PricewaterhouseCoopers LLP. His areas of emphasis are employee benefit plans, investment companies, trust companies, and Statement on Auditing Standards (SAS) 70 reviews of service providers. Mr. Nolan has served on the American Institute of Certified Public Accountants (AICPA) Task Force on the Implementation of SAS 70, and he serves on the AICPA Employee Benefit Plans Committee and the AICPA Task Force on Auditing Financial Instruments.

Bluford H. Putnam is the president of Bayesian Edge Technology & Solutions, Ltd. Formerly, he was the president of CDC Investment Management Corporation and chief investment officer of the Global Investment Management Department at Bankers Trust Company. Mr. Putnam also served as director and chief economist for Kleinwort Benson, principal and head of the international fixed-income strategy team at Morgan Stanley & Company, partner with Stern Stewart & Company, and economist with Chase Manhattan Bank and the Federal Reserve Bank of New York. He has authored several books on international finance, including *Integrating Risk Management into Asset Allocation*, and he writes regularly for the business and academic press. Mr. Putnam holds a B.A. from Eckerd College and a Ph.D. in economics from Tulane University.

Wayne H. Wagner is co-founder and chairman of the board of the Plexus Group, which provides implementation evaluation and advisory services to U.S. and global money managers, brokerage firms, and pension plan sponsors. Mr. Wagner was a founding partner of Wilshire Associates and served as chief investment officer of its Asset Management Division. He has written and spoken frequently on many trading and investment subjects. Mr. Wagner is a regent of AIMR's Financial Analysts Seminar and served on the AIMR Blue Ribbon Task Force on Soft Dollars. He received an M.S. in statistics from Stanford University and a B.B.A. in management science/finance from the University of Wisconsin.

James W. Ware, CFA, is president of Winning with Style, Inc. (formerly known as Jim Ware and Associates), where he delivers workshops and keynote speeches on the role of creativity and collaboration in investing. Mr. Ware's previous money management experience includes research analysis and portfolio management for Allstate Insurance Company and First Chicago. Mr. Ware has published articles in various professional publications, including the *Financial Analysts Journal*. He has taught courses in investing and finance at the Keller Graduate School of Management. Mr. Ware is a member of AIMR's speaker retainer program and delivers speeches on various investment topics to its local chapters around the world. He earned his philosophy degree from Williams College and holds an M.B.A. from the University of Chicago.

Jason Zweig is a columnist at *Money* magazine. His column, "The Fundamentalist," analyzes mutual funds and other investment topics. Previously, he served as a senior editor with *Forbes*, a reporter/researcher for *Time*, and as an editorial assistant for *Africa Report*. Mr. Zweig serves on the editorial advisory boards of several publications, including *Financial History, Journal of Psychology and Financial Markets*, and *Alternative Perspectives on Finance and Accounting* (a forthcoming online journal). Mr. Zweig earned his B.A. from Columbia College and spent a year studying at the Hebrew University in Jerusalem, Israel.

Overview: Ethical Issues for Today's Firm

Some of the most important things in life are taken for granted. Most people assume that the sun will rise tomorrow, that water always flows downhill, and that everyone knows what it means to behave ethically. But knowing what it means to behave ethically and actually behaving ethically can be two quite different issues. A child might know that lying is wrong but still lie about who broke the vase; a thief might know that stealing is immoral but continue to steal anyway; and an investment professional might know that insider trading is illegal but persist in making such trades.

Ethical issues should not be taken for granted in any aspect of life, and the professional world of investment management is no exception. Simply assuming that investment professionals know how to act ethically has gotten many an investment firm into hot water. Part of the reason that ethics is so important in the investment management industry is that investment professionals interact not only with other professionals, who presumably are knowledgeable, but also with the general public (investors), who may have very little knowledge of the workings of the market. The recent bull market has turned the typical U.S. citizen into the typical U.S. investor, and although the bull market has certainly raised the prices of many stocks, in itself it has not raised the knowledge level of investors. If the investment management industry hopes to keep the trust of the investing public, then the industry better be focusing on ethics.

There seems to be a prevailing attitude that discussing ethics (or the lack thereof) in any profession is an admission that the profession has a problem. The fault, in general, lies not with the profession but with the people involved, who are human and who do make mistakes. Nevertheless, if a profession ignores the issue, then the fault does lie squarely with the profession.

Although a few exceptions exist, the investment and finance literature is amazingly silent on the issue of ethics in the industry except when an egregious breach occurs—Nicholas Leeson, Marisa Baridis, and Joseph Jett are a few people whose breaches created a stir in the press. That is a luxury that no profession can afford. The authors in this proceedings have chosen not to remain silent. They address the issue of ethics from two main vantage points: (1) ethics and the industry and (2) ethics and the investment firm.

Ethics and the Industry

Marianne Jennings takes a pointed look at ethics in the investment management industry. She notes that the ethical convictions of people in general are not extremely high. Ironically, the more educated people become, the less ethical they seem to behave. This finding does not bode well for investment professionals, who are almost exclusively highly educated individuals. Jennings stresses that the investment management industry needs to focus on ethics because, to name a few reasons, current laws and regulations are not sufficient to protect against unethical behavior, ethical companies are more successful in the long term than unethical ones, and trust and ethics are the foundation of capital markets—without trust and ethics, investors will stop investing and the markets will cease to function. Finally, Jennings notes that ethical issues should not be placed in an "either/or" construct (e.g., either I do this or I make money). Investment professionals need the courage and creativity to figure out "how to do this and how to make money." Ethical issues do have a right and a wrong answer, and individuals need the conviction to choose the right answer.

A major facet, if not the most important one, of ethics in the investment management industry is the treatment of clients. Jason Zweig challenges investment firms and money managers to treat their clients the way they would like to be treated if they were the clients. Doing so, he believes, will result in treating clients ethically. Along this line of thinking, Zweig asks why tax-efficient investing is not a higher priority; when their own money is involved, money managers surely are concerned about after-tax returns. Similarly, why promote fund performance when the funds are performing extremely well but exactly when returns are most likely to revert to the mean? And finally, why continue to allow new investors (and net new cash flows) into a fund when the size of the fund reaches a nearly unmanageable level? Zweig warns firms that once they lose clients, getting them back will be extremely difficult. Consequently, firms must make an effort to retain their current clients, and one of the best ways of retaining clients is to treat them ethically—as the managers and firms would like to be treated if they were the clients.

James Ware focuses on the gray area of investing and ethics—not the extremes of ethical and unethical where decisions are made relatively easily but the area in the middle where tough decisions need to be made. Ware notes that the investment management industry needs to be concerned about ethics because the public is becoming increasingly concerned about the issue and because one frequent solution to the problem is increased regulation, which rarely solves the underlying problem and creates more work. Part of the problem with ethics in the investment management industry is that a distinction exists (from an ethical standpoint) between investment professionals interacting with fellow professionals and with the investing public. When the interaction is between peers (two professionals), the general feeling is that it is a "fair fight," and thus, they need not be concerned about exploiting each other's knowledge level or feelings about investing. But when a professional is interacting with the typical investor, the professional does need to be cautious not to exploit that individual's knowledge level (which might be quite low) or feelings about investing (which might be very sentimental). In such an interaction, the Golden Rule must be followed.

Ethics and the Investment Firm

The general consensus appears to be that ethics is important in the investment management industry, but how important? Andrew Nolan presents the findings of a survey conducted by PricewaterhouseCoopers about ethics and compliance programs in investment firms. Although 89 percent of the respondents said that an ethics program promotes firm reputation, only 30 percent of firms highlighted their ethics programs in marketing materials. Thus, almost all firms are aware of the importance of an ethics program, but few promote its importance. Not surprisingly, large firms tend to have more formalized ethics and compliance programs than small firms. But one finding that is surprising is how firms learn of policy infringements. Roughly half (44 percent) of the firms said they learn of violations from regulatory inspections and nearly one-third (28 percent) from client complaints. Those firms that find themselves in that one-half or one-third group need to give their ethics and compliance programs increased scrutiny. Nolan also reveals the survey results concerning what areas investment firms consider to be the hot risk areas (such as insider trading) and the current trends in reporting risk controls. Firms that can currently produce such reports have a competitive advantage; those that cannot produce such reports in the next three or four years might find themselves out of business.

Working in the best interests of clients (i.e., working ethically) means paying attention not only to returns but also to costs. Although the commission on trades is one obvious cost, it is far from the only cost. Wayne Wagner discusses quantifying the total trading cost (which includes delay and missed trades) and thus being able to determine if a broker is providing best execution. Trading costs can be measured by using the daily-average method, a similar-trade comparison, or a cost of capture model. Data from the Plexus Group show that the typical cost for a one-way trade on a large-cap stock is 1.01 percent; the one-way cost on a small-cap stock is 4.5 percent. Clearly, costs of such magnitude need to be managed. Another potential impediment to portfolio performance is the use of commission recapture or directed trades. The Plexus Group has found that for easy trades (large-cap stocks in quiet market conditions), the use of commission recapture or directed trades does not impede performance, but hard trades (small-cap stocks in price momentum conditions) should not be done through commission recapture or directed trades. Being sensitive to total trading costs and the effects of using directed trades is as important (and ethically motivated) as thoroughly researching a stock.

Thomas Dillman addresses how to attract, motivate, and retain the best employees, which ultimately leads to superior results for clients. At the core of attracting, motivating, and retaining employees is the firm's culture. How a firm defines itself (the goals and objectives it has, the clients it serves, the products it offers, its organizational structure, and its investment policy) establishes the culture of the firm. And a firm continues to create and modify its culture through its recruiting, training, motivating, and compensation policies. In particular, how a firm measures the performance of its employees has a significant impact on how employees feel about working for a firm—is performance measured fairly, is compensation tied to the performance measures, is good performance rewarded, is poor performance penalized? State Street Research & Management Company uses a combination of quantitative and qualitative measures to assess performance, and Dillman believes in making performance numbers for individuals public knowledge within a firm. Doing so highlights achievements and motivates employees to work hard. Finally, a firm's culture does not (or should not) simply evolve; it needs to be managed to make sure that the ultimate goal is being accomplished—working in the best interests of clients.

Exposing a firm (and the portfolios in its care) to undue risks is neither ethical nor in the best interests of clients. But the key is *undue* risks. Bluford Putnam emphasizes that managing risks does not mean eliminating risks. A certain level of risk is not only appropriate but also necessary to achieve a certain level of return. One of the first steps in managing firm risk is to make real-time and daily net asset valuations on portfolios widely available within the firm. Making such numbers available helps everyone involved in the portfolio process—not just the risk manager or the chief investment officer (CIO)—develop almost a "sixth sense" about the numbers. Looking at such numbers on a daily basis allows those involved to quickly notice a discrepancy in the numbers and alert others to the discrepancy, which is crucial to managing firm risk. Many risk management models and measurement systems originated in the banking industry; however, they are not all appropriate for use in investment management firms. The banking industry and investment management industry approach the investment process differently, which creates differences in what risk management models and approaches are appropriate. Finally, risk management is more than risk measurement and, as such, requires those involved to make judgments and forecasts in order to be of use to portfolio managers and CIOs.

Investment firms that cannot remain competitive will not stay in existence and thus will not be able to work in the best interests of their clients. Charles Burkhart delves into the issue of what makes an investment firm competitive in this day and age. At Investment Counseling, Burkhart and his coworkers conduct an annual survey of firms asking them what makes a firm competitive and successful. The top three answers are asset growth, revenue growth, and profitability. Notice, however, that firm size is not in the top three. Burkhart has found that firm size is one of the least important determinants of success. Another curious finding is that firms rate employee satisfaction very low as a determinant of their success. Burkhart believes that in the future, firms will have to place more emphasis on employee satisfaction; if they do not, they will lose good employees and their ability to compete effectively. The future of investment management, according to Burkhart, will be affected dramatically by the Internet. To be successful (and competitive) in the future, firms will have to marry the old world of investing (the brokers, insurance agents, pension consultants, etc.) with the new world of investing (online brokers, such as E*TRADE Securities; online information sources, such as TheStreet.com; online consultants, such as PlanSponsorExchange.com; etc.). Firms that remain firmly entrenched in the old world will find their competitive edge slipping away.

Conclusion

The investment management industry needs to be concerned about the ethics of the professionals (and firms) in the industry. With more investors who are not particularly knowledgeable about the market entering the market every day, a greater obligation exists for investment professionals to act ethically. And with new financial instruments being engineered every day, investors are relying more and more on investment professionals, thus again creating a greater obligation for investment professionals to behave ethically. The industry, however, needs to do more than talk about being ethical. The industry needs concrete definitions of being ethical and strict ethical codes, and firms need to establish a culture of ethics that encourages all individuals in an investment management firm to work in the best interests of clients—whether that means trying to enhance returns, controlling costs, monitoring risks, or creating an environment where employees work to the best of their ability.

Professional Responsibilities, Ethics, and the Law

Marianne M. Jennings
Professor of Legal and Ethical Studies
Arizona State University

> At the heart of successful markets is trust—an interdependence of business, citizens, government, and investors. Consequently, the investment management industry cannot disregard the importance of ethics. The current state of ethics in the United States is not encouraging; the need exists to focus on ethics, dispel its bad reputation, and learn how to solve ethical dilemmas.

Ethics matter, despite increasing evidence that most individuals do not have strong ethical convictions. Take, for example, an analyst's reaction to the announcement that McCormick & Company was being sued for antitrust violations. In response to the fact that this company would likely face all kinds of fines, the analyst said: "If there is illegal activity going on, I just want to know why I haven't made more money owning the stock."

To me, this is a shocking reaction. The analyst's response suggests that making money and doing something illegal go hand-in-hand. An appropriate analyst response would have been: "I did not know about the illegal activity, and it is not the kind of behavior I tolerate." What is in the best interests of a firm's clients is in the firm's best interests as well.

The McCormick story, unfortunately, is not an isolated case. In this presentation, I will give some compelling business reasons to be concerned with ethics, and I will also try to heighten awareness of the importance of ethics. Even the best of us, particularly in this fast-paced world we live in, lose sight of some obvious issues. We cannot assume that everyone has an understanding of why ethics are important or knows what ethics mean in someone's career or the management of a company.

State of Ethics

Ethical standards tend to deteriorate with increased levels of education. So, in terms of ethics, people are better off with a high school diploma than with a Ph.D. To illustrate the state of ethics for various age groups, I will start with children, move to college students, and then go on to professional life.

According to the Josephson Institute, 90 percent of school-age children have lied to their parents, and 91 percent have cheated at school. A new study puts the level of cheating at 95 percent. The interesting point about these data is how children responded when asked if they had cheated. Their answers have to do with how people redefine rules so that they think they are not really cheating. During one survey, a researcher asked a student if the student had cheated, and the student responded: "Define cheating for me." The researcher said: "If you are sitting in a room and you look at the paper next to yours and copy the answer, that would be cheating." The student said: "No, that would be research." If people redefine how they look at a situation, it often does not look bad or unethical.

The figures on cheating in undergraduate settings are also high. According to a Rutgers University survey, 70 percent of university students have cheated at least once on a test, 87 percent have cheated on written work, and 52 percent have copied work from others.

Another Rutgers University study shows that the majority of students admit to cheating to get into graduate school. Cheating is lowest in liberal arts, but in business schools, 75 percent of students admitted to cheating. A survey came out in the fall of 1998 in which two faculty members compared an ethics test their students took with a test taken by white-collar criminals in prison in Ohio. The prisoners did better in terms of their answers about fraud and such ethical topics.

In the workplace, more than half (51 percent) of those surveyed by the Society for Human Resource Management and the Ethics Resource Center have done, and will confess to having done, something unethical. This statistic is based on a very large survey—6,000 respondents, from the front-line employees to the CEO. The most common form of cheating involved violating quality standards in some way. The second most common form involved lying to cover up a breach in quality. And 36 percent have lied on or falsified a report, from regulatory reports to travel expenses.

A more troubling finding is that most people in the workplace have seen something illegal or unethical during the past year but have said nothing. Sixty-five percent report nothing because the workplace culture is such that they think nobody would take any action or because the conduct has become widely accepted. Other reasons include "nobody cares about it, why should I" and "I didn't trust the organization to keep my report confidential."

The most troubling statistic of all is that 99 percent of those surveyed believed their own ethical standards were higher than those of the people they work with. A 99 percent result is pretty phenomenal, but that result is absolutely *not* true. What it tells me is that people have concerns but have not raised them. People are not talking about the issue.

In the investment management industry, ethics is the most important issue as perceived by members of the profession. Furthermore, a survey of individual investors shows that ethics is the second most important criteria, following performance, for hiring fund managers; one-third of the respondents rated ethics as the most important criteria. A recent survey of auditors who specialize in investment management firms shows that the greatest risk comes from inside the firm, not outside the firm, and that risk relates to ethics (or the lack thereof).

Why Focus on Ethics

Ethically, the "state of the union" is not very good, but more of a reason exists for making a renewed commitment to ethics than the mere fact that we are in bad shape.

Likelihood of Getting Caught. The investment management industry is an industry that has, and continues to enjoy, a fishbowl existence. Everything investment professionals do is watched, observed, criticized, made public, and used for fodder, in many cases, in consumer-type reports. In this environment, the laws of probability do not apply. If someone is not fully honest with clients, does not disclose even something as minor as the level of risk, it will come out. If two people in a company know that they are doing something untoward, it will come out. Every step across that ethical line is subject to public scrutiny.

The laws of probability do not apply here; the issue is one of truth. In the words of the novelist Mark Helprin, truth percolates like a natural force. Despite the odds, ethical risk takers abound—Joseph Jett, Nick Leeson, Long-Term Capital Management, E.F. Hutton—and they get caught.

One of the most striking insights into the soul of someone who drifted so far that she would risk her firm's reputation, her entire professional life, and her personal life comes from Marisa Baridis. Baridis was the "wall": the keeper of the information between the brokerage side of the house and the deal side of the house at Morgan Stanley. By all accounts, she did a great job in her position, except that she sold information to friends for between $2,000 and $10,000, and they traded on that inside information. The U.S. SEC caught on and confronted one of her friends. In exchange for a plea bargain, the friend agreed to wear a wire and meet Baridis one last time. If he could not get her to give a tip, he would lose his plea bargain. In the best way he knew possible, he said: "Marisa, do you understand what you are doing?" She answered: "I know this is like the illegalest thing you can do." Here was someone who was the compliance officer of a firm who understood that she was undertaking the worst form of violation, doing it, and telling her friend about it. Intent was not a problem for the prosecutor.

Companies also stumble without strong ethical cultures. I keep a list of such companies. They are all very fine companies, leaders in their markets, but at the heart of all of their problems are either legal or ethical violations. The result is, for example, Columbia/HCA Healthcare Corporation's 58 percent drop in stock price. The ethical culture of Sears, Roebuck and Company has allowed it to drift from auto center fraud and used batteries sold as new to bankruptcy issues, in which Sears convinced a good portion of the United States that when people declare bankruptcy, their Sears debt is never discharged and Sears can continue to collect it. These companies all paid a price. A $60 million fine, such as that imposed on Sears, is a tough hit for any company. These companies took what they had, including marvelous strategy, good marketing, and good performance, and compromised it by some ethical lapses. They got caught and paid a high price for crossing that line.

Shortcomings of Laws and Codes. As with many professions, the investment management industry has a code of ethics that its members abide by. The industry also adheres to regulations and codified law. The law, however, was never intended to be the maximum. It should be the minimum, but it has been moved down, so that it is now the maximum.

What happens in many fields is the practice of what I call "*Jurassic Park* ethics." The movie *Jurassic Park* has a marvelous summation of how to look at issues ethically. In the movie, a scientist has recreated an extinct form of life in an amusement park, but his investors are nervous. Is this feasible? Is this safe? What is the risk? He brings in a panel of independent scientists to verify the safety of the park. One scientist does not agree with the approach that has been taken and confronts the scientist who created the park: "The thing that I worry about is that you spent so much time asking whether you *could* do this that you forgot to ask whether you *should* do this."

Professional responsibility, fiduciary duties, and law—all those are "could" questions. People, however, need to ask the "should" questions. The following example shows how someone I worked with needed to ask himself the should question. I was a regulator in Arizona, one of the commissioners who regulated public utilities, corporations, and so on for a one-year interim period. Near the end of my term, a filing came in from Tucson Electric Power Company. Tucson Electric Power had found a huge loophole between state and federal law and was going to spin off its generation assets, which were regulated by the federal law, not the state, and thus had the potential to create a great deal more earnings because of the looser federal regulation. If ever there was a sure thing in life, this was it.

A fellow commissioner, whose term was about to expire with mine, said: "As soon as I leave office, I am going to invest in this spin-off." I elected not to invest in it. Could I have done it and been well within the standards of insider trading? Absolutely. From a straight insider-trading perspective, it was a public document. Technically, anybody could have viewed that filing, understood what Tucson Electric Power was about to do, and invested in this company if the person understood regulated ventures.

But "should I have done it?" is a different question. The outcome reveals why that should question was so important. The stock began at $68 a share. It went to $128, $168, and $188, and then it split. My fellow commissioner made a lot of money on that stock, but Tucson Electric Power ultimately had to declare bankruptcy. It had spun off all the asset-rich aspects of the business and left the rate payers with nothing. It was a debacle. Those who invested in the early days of Tucson Electric Power have enjoyed about 10 years of regulatory scrutiny, legislation, and regulation. When the story broke, a headline about my fellow commissioner stated that he used his connections with power companies and abused his public trust to make a lot of money. He did not do so, but perception was everything. Could we do it? Yes. Should we do it? A different question altogether.

Long-Term Success. Another reason that ethics are so important, and few people realize this fact, is that a culture of strong ethics leads to long-term success. Business ethics is certainly not new, but the study of it is relatively new.

Frank Shipper was intrigued by managers who never had an interruption in their careers, and he wanted to see how they differed from those who experienced career setbacks.[1] He thought he would find that the politically savvy ones were the survivors. He gathered his data by questioning these managers, current employees, and past employees (in case there was a disgruntled factor). Two findings emerged. First, the group he studied was enormously diverse in terms of demographics—men, women, all ages and races, and all management styles. Second, the one thing they had in common was that they were described as honest by themselves and current and even disgruntled employees. Employees said that they could rely on these managers for information about the company (even down to something as simple as performance evaluations) and for giving them credit when they had done a job well and notifying senior management about their hard work.

Jacques Werth looked at the characteristics of successful salespeople in his book, *High Probability Selling* (Abba Publishing Company, 1999).[2] His sample included people who had 30-year careers and who were millionaires. He expected to find that these were the type of salespeople who did whatever it takes to close a deal. Instead, he found three things in common: They kept their promises, they practiced full disclosure, and they provided follow-up service. The focus on good, client-based service was part of their success.

My own studies confirm that a relationship exists between long-term survivors in business and ethics. I remember seeing a full-page ad in the *Wall Street Journal* in the 1980s that said "The Diamond Match Company, 100 years of consistent dividends." I was intrigued; I wanted to know if I could find other companies like Diamond Match and, if so, what they had in common. So far, I have found 15 industrial companies that match the profile. Three lessons emerged from my visits with these companies.

First, they are in business to make money. This ethic was found throughout each company. I asked an employee at one of these companies what they were making. He said: "I make money. I make a good product, and I make money." So, the employees knew why they were in business.

---

[1] Frank Shipper, "Ten Qualities of Great Managers," *Wall Street Journal National Business Employment Weekly* (May 25, 1996):1.
[2] See www.highprobabilityselling.com for the first four chapters of this book.

Second, they have what I call the WBAWI (what business are we in) factor. All of the companies diversified, but they knew their business strengths and factored them into their measured risks.

Finally, they all have a very strong sense of values. They not only know why they are in business and what businesses they are in, but they also know what they will and will not do to see their success through. They had a strong sense of values long before someone wrote up codes of ethics. During interviews, four of the CEOs used the term "stewardship," which is a marvelous word with religious connotations, and their mantra was "it is not our money; it belongs to somebody else. We are accountable, and we account to them for that." These companies showed a commitment to ethics.

Studies by Melissa Baucus and David Baucus show the impact on share price of criminal and regulatory missteps made by companies.[3] Most people know that a company's share price drops when a public announcement is made of some type of regulatory or legal sanction. The studies by Baucus and Baucus, however, show a far greater impact on the companies for a far longer period of time than most people would imagine. They discovered that in five years, many of these companies were in bankruptcy and had in no way recovered in terms of earnings or returns. Something is going on in terms of regulatory and legal violations and the performance of a company.

Reputation. A company's capital is its reputation, whether that reputation is its performance or the investor's confidence in the company. A good reputation is a sustainable competitive advantage, and a misstep can cost a company its good reputation. The following sayings illustrate my point:
- The reputation of 1,000 years is determined by the conduct of one hour.
- What goes around comes around.
- A reputation, good or bad, is tough to shake.
- A bad reputation is like a hangover. It takes a while to get rid of, and it makes everything else hurt.

Leadership. Ethics is a leadership tool, which is an important point for the finance industry because it is at a turning point. Ethics as leadership is the ability to look at what is going on in a company and the industry and say: "There is a problem. Let's fix it before we are told how to fix it."

---

[3]M.S. Baucus and D.A. Baucus, "Paying the Piper: An Empirical Examination of Longer-Term Financial Consequences of Illegal Corporate Behavior," *Academy of Management Journal*, vol. 40 (1997):129–151.

Figure 1 shows a typical regulation and litigation cycle. Every issue that is regulated or in litigation today began in the latency stage, where those involved had choices and the law did not tell them what to do. Could they do it? Yes. Should they do it? Different question altogether.

Firms have the opportunity to make all kinds of choices about the type of information they give to clients—information about fees and how they are allocated, for example, which is not dictated by law. A firm can make good choices that enhance the firm's reputation and that build client trust, or it can push the line, in which case the public will become aware of the situation and then the firm moves into regulation/litigation. The absurd part of litigation and being regulated is that an industry becomes regulated if there is enough abuse, even when the regulation does not solve the problem, and it ends up costing firms more to do business. I am advocating a move back to the latency stage, where choices are made voluntarily, but to do that, a strong ethical culture is needed.

The following example shows how regulation did not solve the problem, but better ethics would have. I served as the athletic representative for Arizona State University, which meant I determined the academic eligibility of the student athletes. My assignment from the president of the university was to be the academic conscience of the university and to improve grade point averages (GPAs) and graduation rates for the school's athletes. The job was made harder by the athletic department, which wanted the student athletes to be eligible. The athletic department put a lot of pressure on the athletic representatives to make sure students were eligible by offering rewards, such as tickets to the Super Bowl or the Fiesta Bowl, to the representatives if the student athletes met the eligibility requirements.

I wrote a report describing where Arizona State University was with GPAs and graduation rates so that I could decide if the situation was improving. As part of my responsibilities, I gave the report to the faculty senate, which is subject to open meeting law. The next day, the local newspaper printed the graduation rates and the GPAs of the athletes. The story was not in the sports pages, which is where accomplishments are reported, but on the front page, where shortcomings get reported. The university president called me into his office and said something I have never forgotten: "You may just be a little ahead of your time."

In collegiate sports today, everything is regulated in terms of reporting graduation rates and GPAs. The regulations tell colleges and universities when to

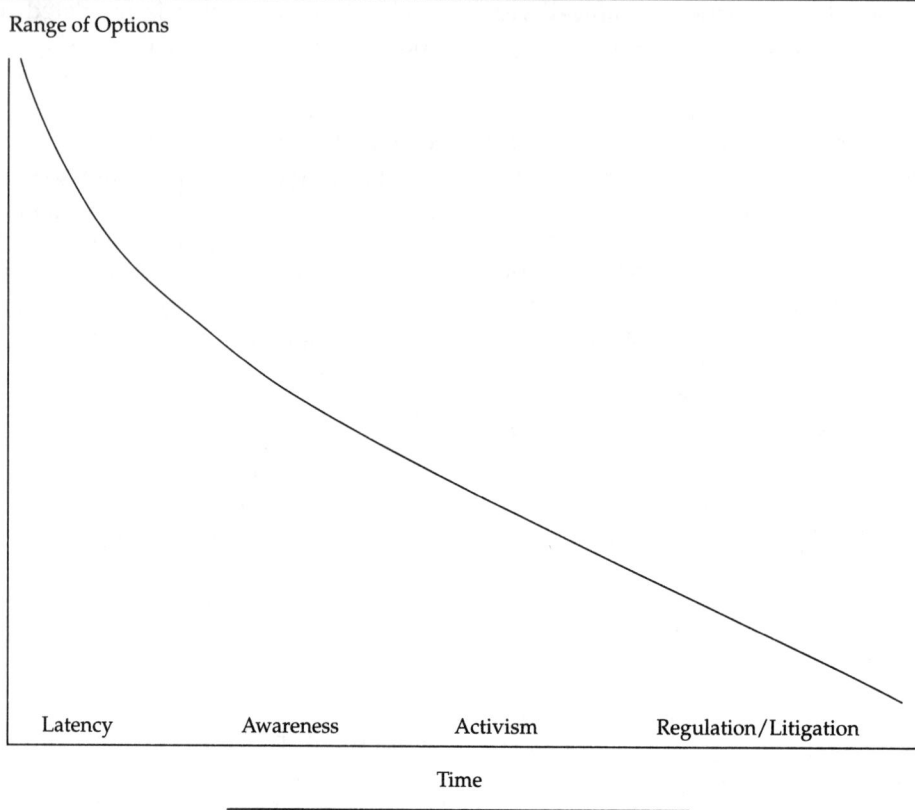

Figure 1. Social, Regulatory, and Litigation Cycle

report the information, how to report it, what the report needs to look like, and when the report is due. A Division I-A school needs to employ one full-time person to comply with the regulations, but the graduation rates and grades are no different from what they were before the regulations came into effect. The schools that were graduating, continue to graduate; those that were not, are not. That is regulation.

The ethical issue is to give these student athletes a chance to succeed outside sports because most of them will not go on to professional sports careers, but colleges and universities are not addressing that ethical issue. Regulation moves in until those ethical issues get addressed.

Morale. A strong ethical culture can serve as a morale booster in a firm. Compliance seems to be the theme in the investment industry, which is wrong. If an industry is emphasizing compliance, it is saying: "Let's get out there and not break the law today." What an industry should say is: "Let's aim for no ill-will among employees, customers, suppliers, citizens, and observers."

Liability. Ethical standards prevent legal difficulties. If an industry is operating by an ethical standard, it is well beyond the law. If people spent more time on the ethics, they would not have to worry about the legal aspects as much.

Market Impact. As people debate microissues with respect to performance and fees, they often forget what is at risk. Ethics is important because it is "the right thing to do." Most people have heard that phrase over and over, and some people would be ethical for that reason alone. But understand that at the heart of successful markets is trust; there is an interdependence of business, citizens, government, and investors. People do not invest because the SEC exists. They invest because they believe the market will function in a certain fashion. They do not invest with the notion that a court will enforce their rights as shareholders. People invest because they understand that underlying assumptions exist in the markets. There is a consensus that fuels the market. Take that trust away and what remains are markets like those in China or Brazil. When a Brazilian official was interviewed about why Brazil's volatility was so high, his response was "Because we are an amoral society. You cannot trust us."

People do not invest when they cannot trust the market, as the following example illustrates. Some friends of mine hosted an exchange student from Macedonia for a year. The host family furnishes room and board for the student, but the student has to bring spending money. This student had been with the family for about two weeks when they realized he had $2,200 in cash that he took in his pocket to school every day. They suggested that he put the money in the bank and withdraw it as necessary, but the concept was literally and figuratively foreign to this young man. He understood contemporaneous exchange: I give you my money, you give me the goods. But he could not understand the notion of trusting someone with someone else's money without that tangible exchange. The family asked what he did at home with extra money, and he said that it goes in a hole in the floor. One can imagine that young man's delight when they explained he would earn interest on his money if he put it in the bank.

Ethics are at the heart of the market, and moral collapse precedes economic collapse. Unless the moral issues are fixed, the United States is headed toward economic collapse because the ethical line is being pushed so far.

Ethics' Bad Reputation

Ethics has a bad reputation for several reasons. First, the urban legend is that you can't get ahead without cutting a few corners. In the investment industry, I hear people say such things as "if I do not do things a certain way, then I am not going to make money." These types of rationalizations are not a realistic look at what people face. People do not have to pick between being ethical and being financially sound.

The second reason ethics has such a bad reputation is that frequently ethics is not enforced. All too often firms are unwilling to enforce the rules in a consistent and swift manner, which is a cultural problem. Sometimes I think people have mixed up the concepts of justice, mercy, and fairness so much that they fail to recognize that misconduct needs to be sanctioned. Employees may need to be let go, and policies may need to change. A lack of enforcement will undermine the commitment to ethics.

Finally, a commitment to ethics is difficult. I am convinced that everyone knows the difference between right and wrong. Everyone knows when they have crossed the line with a client, not disclosed enough information, or not allocated fees properly. Everyone knows the answers. The difficulty lies in execution. Norman Augustine, former chairman and CEO of Lockheed Martin Corporation, is absolutely right: "Not only does one have to know the right thing to do—one needs the moral fortitude to do it."

Ethical Dilemmas

Unfortunately, ethical dilemmas abound. If you find yourself in a situation in which you have to gather your courage to resolve an ethical dilemma, allow me to give you this piece of advice. Do not define your dilemmas by "either/or." I have yet to find an issue in business that boils down to either I do this and I make money or I do not and I do not make money. People have defined situations that way because doing so is expedient. I would ask you to define the situation by the values that you hold and then act on those values, as opposed to using an either/or construct.

Recognizing Dilemmas. Recognizing ethical dilemmas is an important first step in resolving them. One way to recognize ethical dilemmas is to look at any rationalizations you typically make. Rationalizations are not the same as value-based decision making; they are a signal of ethical troubles. Here is a list of typical rationalizations.

- *Everybody else does it, so it must be okay.* That is not a justification; it is a rationalization, and such an attitude has led to practices in the investment industry that have gotten the industry the attention that it has from regulators and others.
- *That is the way they do it at such-and-such firm, so it must be okay.* Do not benchmark your way into ethics; it does not work.
- *If we do not do it, someone else will.* Do what is right. The causes of ethical lapses include job pressures, financial pressures, and political pressures.
- *That is the way it has always been done.* That is the language of rationalization. If you hear that statement, you have a dilemma you have not confronted head on.
- *It does not really hurt anyone.* A lot of actions are rationalized because they will never hurt anyone: soft dollars, churning, B shares, derivatives. Honestly, that statement is not true. Take derivatives, for example. They were marketed without full disclosure of their risks. Now, the entire field is regulated.

Establishing Values. In regard to establishing values, think about what you would want in your employees. What do you deem to be important? Think about values in that context and define them from there. No matter whether I am asking high school students or CEOs, the number one response is honesty. The number two response is integrity. I asked one CEO: "What about competency?" He said: "If employees are honest, I can train them. I just want honest employees."

Next, set some absolutes for yourself. These are the things you will not do to get the firm where it needs to go:
- taking things that do not belong to you,
- telling lies,
- encouraging false impressions,
- creating conflicts of interest, and
- condoning unethical conduct.

All of those areas highlight some of the problems and conflicts in the investment management industry. If you do not draw some absolutes and say, "I am a manager who does not do this," you will cave in. All people have a point at which they compromise their values. The idea is to get as close to that absolute standard as you can, whether you are pragmatic or idealistic, and to avoid the notion of relativism (i.e., deciding on a day-by-day basis what your values are).

I was asked by a reporter about the notion of ethics and why people are slipping so much. The reporter said to me: "Isn't it just because people in business are so evil?" I said that I knew very few people who went into business with the intention to commit a scam but that I knew a lot of people who went into business and moved the line. Moving the line can become so comfortable that before you know it, you have compromised your absolute values. The following example illustrates what can happen when someone moves the line a little at a time.

George Lefcoe, a law professor at the University of Southern California, served as a commissioner in Los Angeles County—a very powerful position in which the individual makes decisions on important issues such as development, permits, and zoning. He went into that job vowing not to accept gifts from the people he regulated. That was his absolute position. The first year, Forest Lawn Cemetery sent him a ham from the HoneyBaked Ham Company. He said that he did not accept gifts and sent it back. Everybody was in a tizzy: "Everybody does this. This is the way it has always been done." He did not understand the ruckus. The next year, when the ham came, rather than deal with the ruckus, he just gave the ham to a worthy charity. The third year, he gave the ham to some worthy friends who did not know he had refused it. The fourth year, he kept the ham but threw a party and invited worthy friends, and by the fifth year, on December 10, he was saying: "Where is my ham?" So, he went from not accepting the ham to the expectation of getting a ham because he moved the line a little bit each year.

Resolving Dilemmas. Resolving ethical dilemmas does not have to be hard or complex. You know the answers to the questions; you just have to face up to them in a business sense. Determining the correct course of action should be easy to discern, as the following examples show.

In the investment industry, the questions to ask are simple. If it were your money or your portfolio, how would you want to be treated? What would you want to know from this investment person? What would you expect that person to disclose? You are wrestling with issues that can be resolved one of two ways: You either do not do it, or you disclose what you are doing to the client. The answer is as simple as that. People try to get far too sophisticated in their analysis.

The so-called Golden Rule "Do unto others as you would have them do unto you," which comes from the Bible, provides a general standard to live by, and the sentiment is universal; it appears in many different religions—from Judaism, to Buddhism, to Islam, to Hinduism—and has been said by many different philosophers—from Confucius, to Aristotle, to Plato. The basic message is the same: Treat people the way you want them to treat you.

A simple test of this principle is the newspaper test. Following news that Salomon Brothers had illegally cornered the bond market, Warren Buffett's advice was that if someone is ashamed to have his or her practices talked about by SEC Chairman Arthur Levitt or put in newspapers, then that person should not follow those practices. If your practices cannot be explained under the public eye, then do not follow them.

On the heels of legal problems with investors, Robert Winters, former chairman and CEO of Prudential Insurance Company of America, said: "If we were making that decision now in light of the press scrutiny we have been receiving, we probably would not have taken that risk." Always assume that you will get press scrutiny. Make up the worst possible headline you can think of, because that is what you will get.

Ken Blanchard, the "one-minute manager," and the late Norman Vincent Peale have this simple test:
- *Is it legal?* If the answer is no, stop there.
- *Is it balanced?* That is, look at the other side.
- *How does it make you feel?* Are you comfortable about this action or decision? This is a question for your conscience.

The *Wall Street Journal* rephrases this test with the three C's: Are you in compliance? What contribution does it make to you, your firm, or your clients? What are the consequences in the long term and short term?

Conclusion

Do not make ethics far more complicated than it needs to be. Disclose. Be honest. Look at issues from the side of the investor. People often say that the client will never understand or that something is for the client's own good. Let clients decide what is for their own good, because that is the ethical posture of honesty and disclosure. Although I said no either/or resolution exists, I want to make an exception in this context. The only either/or decision you should make is either to disclose and be honest or not to disclose and be dishonest. The rest, as they say, is just details.

Question and Answer Session

Marianne M. Jennings

Question: Ethical breaches are a hot topic in the financial press. Why isn't it such a hot topic in the finance literature?

Jennings: There is a bias in the finance literature; ethics is considered so soft and touchy-feely that it irritates most financial editors, but they have to admit that, given the developing studies and literature in ethics, there's something here that is worth a look. So, you're seeing some crossover studies. Most journals have been averse to the discussion of ethics because their focus is so quantitative and market oriented, but I think ethics will start showing up more. For example, I am the guest editor for a special issue of *Corporate Finance Review* (forthcoming in Fall 2000) that is focusing on ethics in finance.

Question: You state that firms should not focus on compliance procedures but, rather, on being ethical. What role should compliance procedures play in a firm?

Jennings: Compliance is the lowest rung on the ethical development ladder. It is but Step 1. Children respond to rules that contain the threat of punishment. As we mature, we learn to understand the reasons for rules, and we comply because we see the bigger picture of rules being in place for our own good. Then, we evolve to the point of caring for more than just our own good, to a point where we care for the protection of the firm, the market, and public trust. Ethics fits in after compliance—it provides the motivation for compliance and the understanding of its role.

Question: How can firms promote better ethics?

Jennings: All officers, managers, and supervisors should be examples of ethical decision makers. Enforce the rules. Draw the line once, and you won't have to draw it for another five years.

Talk about it. Discuss it. Encourage employees to raise issues. Give them a way to raise ethical issues. Reward ethics. Recognize those who do the right thing.

Watch those numbers games. Many a manager has crossed the line to meet goals and postpone the inevitable bad news. Set clear parameters for goals: Define what this firm *will* and *will not* do to achieve them.

You Get the Clients You Deserve

Jason Zweig
Columnist
Money Magazine

> Clients do not want special treatment; they simply want to be treated the same way their investment managers would want to be treated if they were the clients. At the most basic level, a business decision cannot be ethical unless a firm asks not only how something benefits the firm but also how it benefits its clients. If a firm acts only in its own best interests, it will eventually and inevitably act against its clients' best interests.

In the investment management industry, firms seem to believe that they should put their clients on a pedestal, and in fact, I think they do. The typical client on a pedestal, however, bears a striking resemblance to a painting by Antonio Pollaiuolo, circa 1475, called the *Martyrdom of St. Sebastian*. In this painting, St. Sebastian has been carefully placed on a pedestal. In fact, he cannot get off it. The painting depicts this early Christian who was shot full of arrows by Roman soldiers until he resembled a human pincushion.

But in my view, St. Sebastian is also a modern metaphor for the typical investor, the typical client. The painting shows an arrow sticking into St. Sebastian's upper left chest, close to his heart; this arrow might stand for the agony of enormous management fees. Or maybe it represents years of underperforming the market by a margin even wider than the fees themselves—the piercing pain of negative alpha. Perhaps the arrow that is almost completely buried in his belly symbolizes the brutal tax bills generated by excessive portfolio turnover, and the one in the middle of his back might represent an investment management firm that hyped the hot performance of a fund at the exact moment when it was most likely to regress to the mean. The arrow that is sticking in his buttocks probably represents a fund that took in so much cash so fast that it destroyed its own performance, leaving the vast majority of its investors sitting on painfully sharp losses. Finally, the arrow in his right arm might symbolize the way his fund company treats him like an intellectual weakling, bombarding him with boorish marketing materials and inadequate discussions of risk, and the one in his left arm might represent the way his fund company itself behaves like an intellectual weakling, mindlessly herding its way into homogenized portfolios that maximize the firm's own fee income but minimize the chance for active management to live up to its potential.

The painting depicts even more arrows about to hit St. Sebastian. One might be the temptation of day trading, which is often executed by the very same investment firms that keep preaching about investing for the long term. Another might be the notion that getting rich quick is achievable or even desirable. And at least one of the Romans firing arrows into St. Sebastian must be a member of the media; the ethics of my own so-called profession leave much to be desired.

The point is that clients do not want to be put on a pedestal. They simply want to be treated the same way their investment managers would want to be treated if they were the clients.

Ethical Issues

The investment management industry must face four key ethical issues: tax efficiency (or the lack thereof), benchmarking returns, fee explosion, and promoting fund performance.

Tax Efficiency. Fund managers continually claim that they are reluctant to make tax efficiency an explicit objective for their funds. They claim that their goal is to maximize total return and that taxes are secondary. But when these managers invest their own money—when they are the clients—do they seek to maximize their total return pretax or after tax?

Benchmarking Returns. "Style purity," "minimizing tracking error," and "sticking to our discipline" have become articles of faith when money managers sell their services. Yet when they invest their own money—when they are the clients—do they ever pick stocks with the explicit intent of minimizing tracking error? Or are they, instead, trying to earn the best returns they can—with no regard for the benchmark?

Fee Explosion. Investment managers have no qualms about charging more than 1 percent a year to run portfolios that underperform a blindfolded chimpanzee. But when they invest their own money—when they are the clients—would they ever willingly pay more than 1 percent in annual expenses for below-average performance? And would they like to pay the same fees regardless of whether their portfolios perform well or poorly?

The earliest known fund prospectus is for the Foreign and Colonial Government Trust, which is a U.K. fund that was launched in 1868. At that time, expenses were capped at £2,500, which amounted to between 36 and 42 basis points (bps) on the fund's assets for its first five years. This investment trust is still around and performing solidly, and last I checked, its annual expenses were around 47 bps. In well over a century, this fund's expenses have barely budged, but the expenses of U.S. funds have shot up 50 percent in the past four decades, with no end in sight.

It is remarkable that funds advertise their market-beating performance, whenever they have any, and yet they do not charge accordingly. The U.S. SEC allows performance incentive fees, enabling a fund to charge higher fees when it beats a benchmark—so long as it is willing to charge less when it fails to beat it. Nearly every fund sells itself to the public on the grounds that it can or will beat the market, but how many are willing to put their own money on the line and take the other side of the bet they are foisting on the public? According to data from Lipper, the managers of only 158 out of more than 7,700 stock funds (i.e., only 2 percent) are willing to put their own money where their mouths are, and yet they are perfectly happy to encourage their clients to do so. Instead of thinking like clients, the managers are doing the exact opposite.

What is even more offensive is that some fund companies not only ignore their obligation to lower their fees but also believe they have a God-given right to raise them. For example, in 1994, the "independent" trustees of the Putnam High Yield Advantage Fund approved a 27 percent effective hike in management fees for the fund, on which Putnam was already earning a 41 percent net profit margin. Shareholders who voted "no" received an extraordinary letter that stated the following:

> According to our records, you elected to vote against the proposed changes in the management contract. We would like to be sure that you are fully aware of the implications of this decision. The proposal requires approval by 67 percent of the shares voted. If that percentage is not achieved, the meeting will be adjourned until a larger number of shareholders vote their proxies, which, in turn, may end up costing the fund more money for further mailings.

In other words, Putnam was saying that it would continue to charge clients more and more money until they agreed to allow Putnam to charge more and more money. Putnam later apologized for mailing the letter, but its original action made a complete mockery of the term "mutual fund." Would anyone at Putnam ever buy a high-yield bond from a company that treated its creditors this way? Were Putnam's managers treating clients the way they would like to be treated? The questions answer themselves.

Promoting Fund Performance. Mutual funds most heavily promote their performance to the public when performance is at a peak. Mutual fund ads shout "We're number one!" louder than sophomores at a college football game. Yet when fund managers invest their own money—when they are the clients—do they seek out the stocks with the highest past returns, or are they trying to own stocks that will have high returns in the future? No one denies that regression to the mean is the most basic law of financial physics. So, why do funds market to the public as if regression to the mean were nonexistent?

The following example shows what can happen to clients when a fund markets its performance at its peak. Parnassus Investments advertised that it had the number one growth fund in America. When I looked at data from Lipper to see how the fund performed in subsequent periods, I found that America's number one growth fund over the succeeding five quarters turned out no longer to be America's number one growth fund. The people who already owned America's number one growth fund enjoyed good returns, at least for a while, but the people who bought it on the basis of its number one performance got the 874th growth fund or the 881st growth fund.

The Great Divide

Those four ethical issues all stem from the artificial divide the investment management industry has erected between advisors and clients. To be blunt, business decisions cannot be ethical unless a firm asks not only how something benefits the firm but also how it benefits its clients. If a firm acts only in its own best interests, it will eventually and inevitably act against its clients' best interests.

In fact, to define "ethics" in any other way than acting in the best interests of others is to define the term into meaninglessness. As John Stuart Mill wrote in *Utilitarianism* in 1861:[1]

> The interest of mankind collectively, or at least of mankind indiscriminately, must be in the mind of the agent when conscientiously deciding on the morality of the act.... we ought to shape our conduct by a rule which all rational beings might adopt *with benefit to their collective interest*. (p. 49)

The term is "mutual fund," not "fund."

One of Wall Street's wisest sayings is, "You get the clients you deserve." If firms do not acknowledge at the outset, and in every day and at every hour, that everything they do must serve their clients' best interests as well as their own, then firms are doomed to deserve the kinds of clients no one wants. To deserve the clients firms would like to have, they must treat clients as they would expect to be treated if they were clients. More basically still, they need to act more like clients.

Now more than ever, acting like a client is not only an ethical imperative but also a business imperative. In today's Internet world, if firms do not serve their clients well, clients will serve themselves. The illusion of free investing on the Internet, and the high visibility of "the big score," is becoming irresistible. Try telling someone whose "dot com" stocks are up 173 percent in the past eight months that he is just lucky and could really benefit from professional stock-picking ability. It does not matter that the only thing this person knows about his stocks is their ticker symbols, or even that he owns QXT when he meant to buy QZT. From his point of view, he is a genius who is getting rich quick, which is fun and free; why on earth should he pay someone outlandish fees to lag the S&P 500 Index every year?

If this bull market lasts for several more years, individual investors may get to the point where they no longer add any money to mutual funds, except in their 401(k)s. If the stock market stays strong, I am gravely concerned that the mutual fund industry—aside from its sheltered position as the default choice for retirement plans—will end up squandering its natural role as the greatest contribution to financial democracy ever devised. Instead, it will become a quaint artifact. Fund companies will only be able to win back clients once they suffer a severe bear market—a marketing task about as easy as being chief recruiter for the Linda Tripp Fan Club. Even when day trading is finally recognized as the low-rent Las Vegas that it really is, guess what fund companies will still have to contend with: the index fund monster, which is going to loom over the landscape no matter what happens, continuing to make funds look bad in all but their best years and relentlessly draining off their institutional clients.

The Good Old Days

The investment management industry all too easily underestimates the anger of the investing public. A recent Securities Industry Association press release boasted that a mere 42 percent of the investing public believes the securities industry is "motivated by greed." The release proudly pointed out that that figure was "down from 49 percent in 1998 and 55 percent in 1997." This optimism is like looking at a glass that is half empty and declaring that it is completely full—and what it is full of is not drinkable either.

I get several dozen e-mails a week from retail investors, and they are fed up with the way this industry treats them. The main (although far from the only) reason the public is so disgusted is because of poor relative performance. The narrowness of the market in recent years accounts for much of that performance issue, and firms are right to explain it to their clients. But the situation is getting worse. The people who say that portfolio managers' jobs will get easy (like the good old days) just as soon as the market broadens again are wrong.

The good old days are gone forever, and here is the reason why. In the past, the investor who got the earliest grasp on the best information earned the highest return. The classic example is Nathan Rothschild and his flock of carrier pigeons, which almost 200 years ago gave him the finest early warning system in Europe and enabled him to dominate the foreign currency and bond markets for decades. In that kind of environment, the commodity that could be arbitraged most profitably was time itself.

But today, virtually every bit and byte of market information is transmitted instantaneously to every investor everywhere on earth. A great deal of information, in fact, is old before it even exists. Once upon a time buy-side analysts spent weeks painstakingly calculating their own earnings estimates; today, what counts is "whisper numbers" and even "prewhispers." Weeks in advance of any actual earnings release, the future has already been decided, and these numbers, which used to be an institutional commodity, now hit the Internet in a flash, for the whole world to see.

Meanwhile, fund performance—which used to be measured annually, then quarterly, then monthly—is now measured daily. In 1959, the typical fund owned its stocks for six years, on average. In 1999, the average holding period of stock funds will probably drop

---

[1] John Stuart Mill, "Utilitarianism," in *Utilitarianism, On Liberty, and Considerations on Representative Government* (London: J.M. Dent & Sons, 1977). Italics in the original.

below 12 months—the lowest, I believe, that it has ever fallen. Millions of investors, retail and professional alike, track stocks in real time, tick by tick, and soon they will be trading 24 hours a day. A recent article in the *Journal of Financial Economics* found that day trading is most profitable for holding periods of 80 seconds or less.[2]

Thus, the long term has shrunk down to anything longer than 1.5 minutes. Time is no longer arbitrageable. The velocity of learning has hit warp speed, and the informational efficiency of the stock market has never been higher. Professional money managers have lost the exclusive and powerful advantage that time arbitrage once gave them; scarier still, they have become the victims of it.

Research shows that the value of a reward is related to the length of time remaining until the reward can be obtained. The curves in **Figure 1**—which are based on experiments conducted on many species, ranging from rodents to birds to insects to humans—plot how the perceived or subjective value of each reward changes as time passes. This figure shows that when the time to receive a reward is in the distant future (in the region of t_2 on the figure), the larger, more remote reward is more attractive (i.e., has a higher value). But when the time to receive a reward is shorter (in the region of t_1), then the smaller, closer payoff becomes far more preferable. Where the lines cross is what psychologists call "preference reversal."

Think of the situation this way: When you are hungry, would you rather eat a large meal several hours from now or a small meal right now? The answer is obvious: When time is compressed, short-term, partial gratification becomes more satisfying than long-term, fuller gratification. This finding makes the pursuit of any long-horizon strategy—such as, say, a deep-value approach—psychologically painful, both for the firm and its clients. Clients want to eat now, not later, and so do firms. And as the Internet and CNBC and information saturation become universal, any investment strategy that does not pay off for years becomes almost unendurably difficult to promote.

Besides the acceleration of time, the power of the bull market is adding to this pressure. In an up market, what is a loss? The answer is not "losing money"

---

[2]Jeffrey H. Harris and Paul H. Schultz, "The Trading Profits of SOES Bandits," *Journal of Financial Economics* (October 1998):39–62.

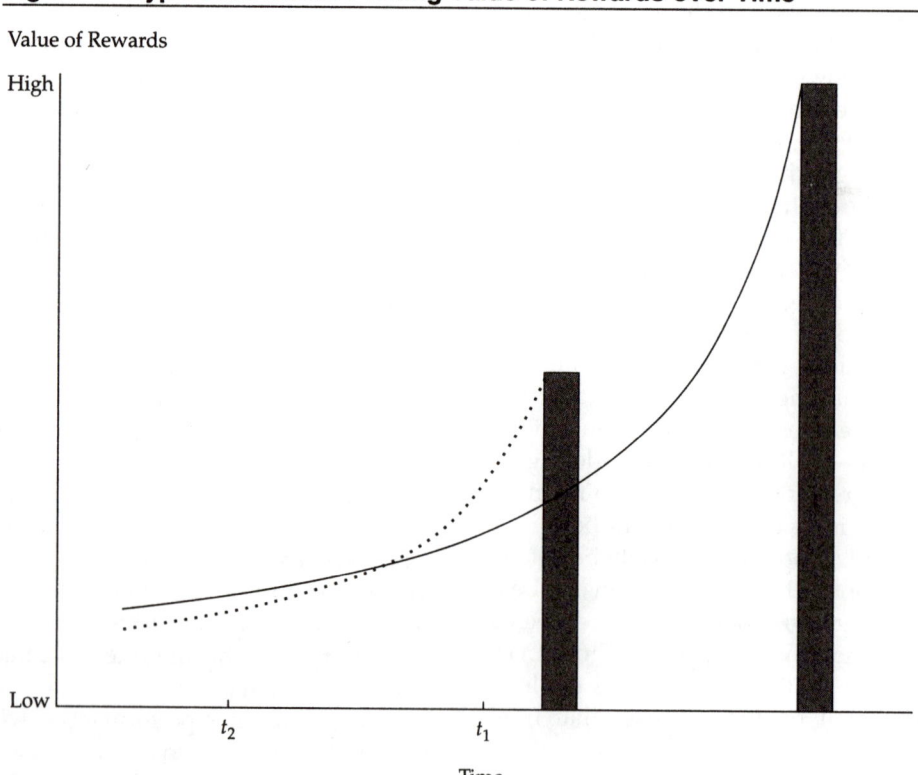

Figure 1. Hyperbolic Model Plotting Value of Rewards over Time

Source: Leonard Green and Joel Myerson, "Exponential versus Hyperbolic Discounting of Delayed Outcomes: Risk and Waiting Time," *American Zoologist* (September 1996):496–505.

but "making a little less." And when investors see risk not as a true loss but merely as a foregone gain, they have an easy time dumping investments. Instead of kicking themselves, they can kick the portfolio managers—right out the door. Thus, for clients, firing a manager is not a damaging admission of their own fallibility; after all, they made some money instead of losing it. So, they are playing with the house money, which makes firing the manager easier than ever. Forget the old days, when fund investors used to need a signature guarantee before they could even write a letter to the transfer agent requesting a redemption, which took seven business days to settle. These days, three mouse clicks and they are gone.

In light of this changing investor sentiment, avoiding tracking error has become the prime directive, and relative performance has assumed absolute importance.

Retaining Clients

Because clients are so willing and able to leave firms, excellence in investment management no longer depends on getting the best information first, or hiring the smartest people, or building the best software. It depends, more than it ever has before, on a firm's ability to retain its clients—not to *obtain* them but to *retain* them.

Thus, how a firm chooses to market its investments is not just a vital business decision but an ethical decision as well, which surprises a lot of people. Most investment managers think ethics means establishing and living by fair rules of investing conduct, but in today's marketplace, how a manager invests funds and markets funds have become inseparable. Let me illustrate the point with examples.

Example One. From mid-1992 through the end of 1995, a leading small-cap mutual fund more than doubled in value, with little to no impact on the amount of assets under management. Monthly cash inflows during the period ranged from zero to less than zero to slightly more than zero. But then it became number one for capital appreciation over the trailing 3, 5, and 10 years, and its managers yodeled that number one ranking at the top of their lungs in advertisements far and wide. Advertising this number one ranking was like rubbing raw meat across a lion's nose. The public did not just invest in this fund; it attacked it. At the end of 1992, the fund had total net assets of just $3 million. In the first six months of 1996, it took in $2.5 billion.

And then small caps corrected, the fund's returns tumbled, the manager had to panic-sell into a dropping market, and the public yanked out its money. Because the manager's actions aided and abetted the public's own worst behavior, the public investors in this fund suffered dramatically. Although this fund had beaten the market by nearly two to one and nearly tripled in value from 1992–1997 with a time-weighted return of 27.68 percent, it earned an average of only 3.63 percent on an asset-weighted basis, or less than half the return of a certificate of deposit. Today, the fund's assets, which peaked at $6 billion in the height of the public feeding frenzy, languish below $3 billion. And its returns went from the top of the heap to the bottom.

By heavily promoting its performance when it was hottest—exactly when regression to the mean had the highest potential to destroy investors' wealth—this fund's managers treated clients like strangers rather than partners. Managers who think like clients would never behave this way. Poetically enough, in the end, these managers ended up not only devastating their clients but nearly destroying their own business. When I say that you get the clients you deserve, I am not kidding.

The lesson here is unavoidable. The cash flow from clients now rivals the investment process itself as the main determinant of total return. Asset elephantiasis can pulverize returns even worse than a market crash can. Unlike the profitability of their stock picks, firms *can* control the rate at which cash flows into their funds, and the decision to control cash flow is an ethical choice. I would argue, in fact, that it is one of the most important ethical choices any investment firm will ever face.

Example Two. Several years ago, a small-cap manager with a distinguished long-term record went to his firm's management committee asking that his fund be closed to new investors. As he told me:

> We'd gone from maybe $40,000 a day in net cash flow to $6 or $8 million a day, and I could no longer put the money to work in stocks I was comfortable with. When I asked [the management committee] to cap the fund, they said, "We can't close it. It's the only thing we've got that's selling." I saw myself being diluted into mediocrity, so I quit.

The thousands of shareholders who bought this fund because they wanted their money managed specifically by this man were out of luck. Even worse, the fund manager was forced to quit his job precisely because he was thinking like a client, precisely because of his belief that his firm had to consider the best interests of its clients in addition to its own.

Example Three. Here is another case of a manager—in this case a bond manager—putting himself in his clients' shoes only to find that one of the firm's directors was showing complete contempt for the firm's clients. Here is his chilling story:

> At a board meeting at my former firm, an independent director said to me, "You should stop focusing on long-term returns—don't you know that short-term performance is the name of the game for gathering assets these days?" I couldn't believe my ears. I asked him if he meant short-term, like monthly returns. The director said, "That's right." And that is why I left to work at another firm.

Example Four. A couple of years ago, I saw a bright, customized greeting card, festooned with colored streamers, that a rapidly growing fund company had sent to its existing shareholders asking them to "Join us in celebrating the reopening of [the fund]." These shareholders had nothing to celebrate and everything to mourn. The firm they had entrusted with their hard-earned money was not only acting against their best interests but also treating them as if they were too stupid to know the difference.

Summary. One of the odd things about being a journalist is that people are always willing to tell me the truth—but only if I agree not to print it. I have met portfolio managers who would deny on the record that rapid and massive asset growth is bad for their existing shareholders. But I have never yet met a fund manager who denied it off the record. The faster the fund gets bigger, the higher the transaction costs, the harder it becomes to find stocks the manager likes, the more stocks the manager is forced to own, and the less the manager knows about any of them. The truth is that the indiscriminate addition of new clients is bad for existing clients. The pursuit of rapid asset growth for its own sake, for a firm's own sake, cannot be defended on ethical grounds because it is directly against the clients' best interests.

Redefining Goals

What, then, should firms be doing? The traditional definition of high achievement for an investment management firm is to outperform a benchmark. I would like to propose a complete and radical redefinition: The highest ethical role of an investment management firm is not to earn the greatest possible return but to do everything in its power to ensure that *each of its clients* earns the greatest possible return. A firm's ethical imperative is to reduce the gap between the time-weighted returns of its portfolios and the dollar-weighted returns of its clients—to do its best to help every one of its clients earn the maximum possible proportion of the returns that the firm generates over time.

When a firm hypes a portfolio at the point of maximum performance, clients suffer for several reasons. First, the firm raises the odds that regression to the mean will have agonizing consequences for its newest clients. Second, the firm all but ensures that its results will regress to the mean, as the weighty force of cash flow crushes returns. Third, firms are committing a peculiar kind of performance suicide, in which their investors die and their management fees live on. Although a firm's time-weighted returns will often seem respectable, its average client will earn a miserable return. This tragedy will go unreported and unnoticed, because no one publishes dollar-weighted returns, but the cover of darkness is no defense.

In a recent issue of *The Ambachtsheer Letter*, Keith Ambachtsheer asked:[3]

> Should an explicit AIMR goal be to reduce the informational asymmetry between the sellers and buyers of investment management and research services? If the answer is "yes," what strategies would be most effective? (p. 3)

In my view, reducing the informational asymmetry between those who sell investments and those who buy them must be an explicit AIMR goal. By doing so, firms can narrow the shameful gap between the time-weighted returns of their portfolios and the dollar-weighted returns of their clients. As André Perold and Bob Salomon brilliantly wrote:[4] "Rather than rate of return, the goal should be the maximization of the total dollar return—the total wealth the investment process is capable of creating" (p. 31).

I like to tell the following little parable about the bus I ride to work each morning to illustrate my point about redefining goals. One day I asked the bus driver, "How many people ride your bus all the way from the first stop to the last?" "Nobody does that," he said. "Matter of fact, nobody ever *has* done that." A portfolio is just like a bus. The only person who rides it for the whole trip, and earns the full measure of the wealth it can generate, is the driver. The passengers all get on and off far too quickly; most of them never even get near where they want to go. But a mutual fund is worse than a bus in one respect: The bus driver never eggs the passengers on to the bus at the worst possible time, nor does the driver throw them off just when they would be best advised to stay. I submit that the portfolio manager's job is to do everything in his or her power to keep as many passengers as possible riding the bus for as long as

---

[3] Keith P. Ambachtsheer, "Is AIMR Too 'Sell-Side'?" *The Ambachtsheer Letter*, no. 166 (K.P.A. Advisory Services Limited: Toronto, Canada, October 29, 1999).

[4] André Perold and Robert S. Salomon, Jr., "The Right Amount of Assets Under Management," *Financial Analysts Journal* (May/June 1991):31–39.

possible. Get them on the bus, keep them on the bus, and ride right alongside them: That is the essence of ethical behavior for an investment manager.

Communication

One simple way to achieve this goal of "riding alongside clients" is to use better communication. I am often asked how active management can fight back in the battle against indexing. The easy answer—"Just beat the market, pal"—is the wrong answer. Instead, what I advise active managers to do is something that a bloodless, faceless index fund can never do: Build a community.

The people at Southeastern Asset Management, who run the Longleaf funds, work on building a community. On the very first text page of its prospectuses, Southeastern Asset Management states what it stands for:

> We will treat your investment in Longleaf as if it were our own. . . . We will remain significant investors with you in Longleaf. . . . We will invest for the long term. . . . We will consider closing the Funds to new investors. . . . We will discourage short-term speculators. . . . We will communicate with our investment partners as candidly as possible.

In themselves, such statements have no value. The firm has to believe them, it has to mean them, and it has to show its clients that it means them. Each May, Longleaf holds a shareholder meeting in Memphis, Tennessee. The advisor, not the fund, pays for this event, and in 1999, more than 400 people came. One couple comes all the way from San Diego, California, every year; another man rides a motorcycle down from Allentown, Pennsylvania. The fund managers—and the independent directors—do not just give formal speeches; they let individual clients come right up to them, face to face, like equals talking to equals, just as the fund managers would like to be treated if they were clients. And, of course, they are clients; the people who run Longleaf have more than $200 million of their own money in their own funds. Maybe that is where some of the sincerity in the prospectus comes from.

Another example of treating clients right comes from an ad for a Warburg Pincus fund. The ad discloses that the fund actually underperformed the S&P 500, and it warns of an upcoming tax distribution. This is intelligent and fair risk disclosure.

One tiny fund company is using the Internet wisely and well. Robert Loest, CFA, who runs the IPS Millennium Fund, has tackled the problem of teaching people about risk. When people go to the IPS Millennium Web site (www.ipsmillennium.com) and click on the link for information about the IPS Millennium Fund, they can choose between reading "Risk Disclosure: Human Language" or "Risk Disclosure: Legal Boilerplate." The "Human Language" is charming, funny, and highly effective. Following is an excerpt:

> While the long-term bias in stock prices is upward, stocks enter a bear market with amazing regularity, about every 3–4 years. It goes with the territory. Expect it. Live with it. If you can't do that, go bury your money in a jar or put it in the bank and don't bother us about why your investment goes south sometimes or why water runs downhill. It's physics, man.

Not only does a prospective client get an entertaining discussion of risk but also a real sense of what the person who runs this fund is like and how he thinks, which is the first step in building a community.

Ten-Step Program

What are the best ways that as an investment manager you can get clients on the bus, keep them on the bus, and ride alongside them? In the spirit of a good personal-finance journalist, let me offer 10 great ways you can do better.

One. Ask yourself a basic question: Are you better off voluntarily reducing your fund's expenses now, when you can afford it, or waiting until the markets fall, when your high fees will stick out like a sore thumb? I submit to you that if you wait, you face only two choices: cut your fees at the bottom of the market or lose shareholders to the firms that already have cut them.

Two. Require, across the entire firm, that all bonus compensation and all retirement plan assets be reinvested in your own funds. Then disclose this policy, and disclose, in percentage terms if you prefer, how much of each fund the firm's executives, employees, and directors own. There is simply no better way to align your interests with those of your shareholders than by investing alongside them as partners. Acting in your clients' best interests is far easier once you are among your own largest clients.

Three. Ask whether an optimal asset size exists beyond which each portfolio should not be allowed to grow. (Once the firm's own staff has its own money substantially on the line, this question will be a lot easier to answer.) Then tell your clients in advance that you have set a ceiling for asset growth, and tell them why. That disclosure will teach them something about investing and something about the character of your firm.

Four. Define what you do much more clearly. If some clients demand minimal tracking error, then give it to them. But segregate that money where it cannot infect the rest of your accounts with its lack of ambition. Live up to the meaning of the word "firm"; stand firm, and do not get caught up in a race to the bottom. Likewise, if the 401(k) market is important to you, then add an index fund to your lineup; let that fund be the main receptacle for the 401(k) cash flow so that it cannot swamp the success of your other accounts. And if some of your funds are managed with little or no regard for tax consequences, then say so; tell your clients where you are tax efficient and where you are not. Your job is to disclose; a client's job is not to try to figure out.

Five. Call a complete halt to performance advertising. "We're number one!" works in the short run. But you know how regression to the mean works. Do not inflict mean-regressing returns on other people; it is just not right. What is more, acting in such a manner gets you what you deserve. The shareholders who buy your funds when they are momentarily ranked number one or temporarily emblazoned with five stars will always be LIFO (last in, first out) shareholders. When performance turns, they will desert you at the drop of a hat.

Six. Reward your shareholders for good behavior. People have grown to expect frequent flyer miles as the natural reward for loyalty to an airline or special prices at the grocery store when they use their savings club card. Why not pay your loyal long-term shareholders a small year-end bonus—say, 10 bps of their account value, automatically reinvested in new shares? The new exchange fund in Hong Kong is doing exactly this, issuing bonus shares for loyal investors who hang on for the long term, which, of course, in Hong Kong is one year or more.

Seven. Emphasize the human touch. Besides Longleaf, a few other fund groups hold annual meetings for their clients. For a few thousand dollars, the advisor gives hundreds of shareholders the opportunity to build an emotional bond with the fund and its managers. Loyalty is a two-way street. If you train your clients to think of your funds merely as mechanical generators of raw return, rather than as a community of people with mutual interests, their loyalty will always be as perishable as your performance. I am baffled that the industry uses the term "fund family" with no sense of embarrassment. What kind of family is made up of people who have never even met each other and are actively prevented from doing so by the master of the household? Simply by letting clients meet their portfolio manager and shake his or her hand, these few innovative firms are encouraging their clients to be loyal for years to come, and they are enabling active management to live up to its potential. These managers are teaching their clients, face to face, the power and value of long-term investing. The fund industry sees with its own eyes that Warren Buffett can fill a stadium at his annual meeting, but most fund managers yawn and look the other way. A few rare firms, however, have begun building a powerful emotional bond with their clients, and when the great bear market finally comes, these firms will retain a far higher share of their clients than the ones that have not established such a bond.

Eight. Use the Internet imaginatively and often to grab clients with short attention spans but intense interest. Set up live question and answer sessions for your portfolio managers once a month. Do as the IPS Millennium Fund did, and teach your clients about risk in a way that is fun and unforgettable. Tackle the problem of the wildly inflated expectations for future returns; tell your clients what you really think. Nobody reads a prospectus, but everybody is getting online. Good risk disclosure no longer has to be boring, which is a huge breakthrough and is ethically important. Do not let the opportunity pass you by!

Nine. The system of mutual fund independent directors needs a lot of toughening up. Too many independent directors, like the one I mentioned earlier, think that their job is to make the investment advisor rich. They sometimes forget about the client altogether. Chris Tobe, a CFA charterholder in the Kentucky State Auditor's Office, has proposed that AIMR encourage the establishment of a pool of unaffiliated CFA charterholders who would serve as independent fund directors, with the specific responsibility of reporting on the fairness of fees and other ethical issues. It is a proposal worth thinking about. I would suggest an even simpler alternative: Ask yourself whether your portfolios are run under the same strict standards of corporate governance that you expect from the companies you invest in. A double standard is no standard at all. If your own corporate governance falls short by this test, then go out and recruit the toughest, most combative business leader you can find and put him or her on your board. Tell him or her to defend your clients' best interests whenever you forget to.

Ten. Use performance fees. Stop asking your clients to take a bet that you are refusing! If you think they should bet their money on your ability to beat the market, then you darn well should bet your own money too. I am shocked that some fund companies pay portfolio managers bonuses based on the size of assets and the volume of positive cash flow into their funds, while out of the other side of their mouths they lead their clients to believe that beating the benchmark is the name of the game. The best way to cure this conflict is with contingent performance fees. As Max Bazerman and James Gillespie recently wrote in the *Harvard Business Review*, "Using a contingent contract to share risk often has an important additional benefit: It creates enormous goodwill . . . [and] tends to enhance the trust between the parties."[5] By showing your clients you are putting your own money where your mouth is, you send them a powerful signal that you are on their side.

---

[5] Max H. Bazerman and James J. Gillespie, "Betting on the Future: The Virtues of Contingent Contracts," *Harvard Business Review* (September–October 1999):3–8.

Conclusion

Ultimately, ethics in investment management is about serving clients' best interests, and for firms to do so, they have to think like their clients. To think like their clients, they need to *be* clients. Putting clients' best interests first does not mean putting a firm's own interests last. It simply means aligning the firm's own best interests with clients'. In the end, both the firm and the clients will be better served, and I venture to say both sides will even make at least as much money in the long run.

One final thought: St. Sebastian was not killed by all the arrows that the soldiers fired into his body. He lived on, to fight again. In the long run, firms will get the clients they deserve. I hope firms will try as hard as they can to deserve only the very best clients.

Question and Answer Session

Jason Zweig

Question: Why is the issue of ethics important?

Zweig: The issue is important for the very reason that we have securities regulations. If ethics did not matter, we would not have securities laws. To put ethics on the back burner is understandable in a bull market. But I would argue that during markets like these, ethics is more important than it normally is because when the market does ultimately come apart, we will find out where all the problems were. I had an aunt who used to say that it is not until the rinse cycle that you can see how dirty the laundry really was. I think that is what we're going to find when the bear market does finally come, whenever that is.

Maintaining the investment public's confidence in the securities markets is the single most important issue that any investment firm faces. You can't divorce that basic goal from a devotion to higher ethics.

Question: What is the problem with focusing on tracking error?

Zweig: Clients may sometimes demand things that make you uncomfortable, and if I were an active manager, I don't think I would really appreciate being told that my prime directive was to minimize tracking error, because I would think my prime directive would be to maximize return. It is not purely an ethical issue but also a matter of business judgment.

I think the proper response is to define yourself more clearly, as I mentioned. If you have clients, especially institutional ones, who insist on minimizing tracking error, then you can give them that service. But you might want to keep that money separate so that you can show elsewhere what you really can do.

Question: What do you recommend for improving the governance of mutual funds?

Zweig: I think that Chris Tobe's idea of some sort of ombudsman role might go some ways toward improving mutual fund governance, but it is a very difficult problem. The system of independent mutual fund directors is probably the single worst flaw in the Investment Company Act of 1940. Independent mutual fund directors have a great deal of difficulty acting in a way that most of us would recognize as independent. Because these people are appointed by someone, they believe that person to be their boss, when, of course, he or she is not. Under law, that person is not the boss, but what is true *de jure* is not true *de facto*. This person appointed these directors, they get paid pretty well, and they get to go golfing in a lot of nice places. Generally, they are going to do what they are told, which is a difficult problem and not an easy one to resolve.

My point was that the best way to get people to think like clients is not by telling them to think like clients but by requiring them to be clients. If you look at proxies, you will see that mutual fund directors generally have lower ownership stakes in mutual funds than corporate directors do in the companies whose boards they serve on, which is partly because mutual fund directors tend to have overlapping directorships. The problem could be changed with better bylaws, simply requiring within the firm that a director must invest a minimum of x in the company's fund shares.

Question: What's your reaction to the plain English initiative for prospectuses?

Zweig: Like a lot of regulatory initiatives, it has been overtaken by the real world marketplace. Just as the SEC tried to come up with a mathematical formula that would work as a form of risk disclosure, its efforts were eclipsed by better risk disclosures by mutual funds. The plain English initiative is a good idea, and fund companies are finally getting the point, as evidenced by such documents as those from the IPS Millennium Fund. The SEC is now getting out of the way and letting capitalism work, allowing intelligent people to come up with better ways to approach an audience.

Question: Do you foresee a decline in the demand for active management?

Zweig: So long as the bull market lasts, yes. But the flip side is that I don't think you should be too complacent. Although the conventional wisdom is that when the market finally goes down, active management will redeem itself, I think that is being too optimistic. History tells me that active management, despite all our intuitions to the contrary, does not work any better in a bear market or a flat market than it does in an up market.

What will change in a bear market is that the people who are flipping mutual funds and stocks on their own will learn that they do not have any special security-picking ability. But active managers are going to have a hard time winning those people back because they will be disgusted with equity investments in general. They're not going to view active managers with any special regard just because they themselves made a mistake. What we learned in the 1970s is that when people lost massive amounts of money, they often didn't get back in the market for a decade. And the reason wasn't because active management was doing poorly; it was because they had been burnt.

Winning investors back will be very difficult, which is why it is so important while the market is still strong to keep the shareholders you have, your clients, and to put loyalty measures in place before it is too late. Once clients go out the door, you will have a terrible time getting them back.

Question: Is something happening among the investing public that is an inevitable wave of change?

Zweig: My hunch, based on history, is that when the bull market finally does stop—and we will all know when it happens because suddenly people will be talking about risk again—the idea will go away that getting rich quick is a legitimate and sensible investment goal. People will care again about preserving capital.

What can firms do about it in the meantime? They can build client loyalty now before it's too late. For a very small firm, bringing in new clients may be vitally important, but large firms should focus far more on client retention at this point than getting new clients, because once clients go away, getting them back will be incredibly difficult. In the 1970s, a period when the market was fairly dormant, one-third of all funds in existence disappeared, but more importantly, one-third to one-half of all the shareholders disappeared.

Drawing the Line in a Gray Area

James W. Ware, CFA
President
Winning with Style, Inc.[1]

> Although people may disagree about what is ethical and what is not, establishing and maintaining ethical standards in the investment management industry is of paramount importance. Clients and managers are not always on a level playing field, and the potential for a manager to cross the line and exploit clients' lack of experience can lead to many ethical quagmires. Thus, agreeing to play by the rules is the only way for managers to uphold their fiduciary responsibilities, not to mention to avoid overregulation.

Ethics is at the core of a healthy industry because a healthy industry requires a level playing field and clear understandings. In the investment business, the playing field is not level, especially when professionals deal with the general public. Clients are disadvantaged either because of their attitude toward investing (overly trusting) or knowledge (limited) or both.

Making ethical decisions is relatively easy at the extremes. Who would consider it ethical for a money manager to take clients' money and put it in his or her own back account? And who would consider it unethical for a money manager to disclose to his or her firm that a fellow employee was embezzling firm money? But the gray area—the area between black and white, the place where reasonable people disagree, the place where, as Woody Allen once said, "I feel strongly both ways"—is perhaps the most difficult area in ethics to manage. In this presentation, I will explore why ethics (in particular the gray area) is important to investment professionals, address what can be done about the state of ethics, and give some actual examples of the gray area.

Why Care?

In investing, many ethical swamps—soft dollars, insider trading, fiduciary duties—exist. The immediate and important question, though, is: Why should people care? Why should people spend their valuable time investigating a soft issue such as ethics? The response to this soft question is a hard answer, delivered recently in a *Wall Street Journal* editorial:

"Whatever the standards of the White House, Wall Street needs higher sights.... Capitalism only works well when folks play by the rules."[2] Luckily, corporate America is becoming more aware of the importance of ethics. The percentage of companies with an ethics code has risen from roughly 20 percent to roughly 80 percent between 1987 and 1998.

Regulation is often the solution to unethical behavior, but again, as quoted in the *Wall Street Journal*, "reactive regulation, as opposed to a careful balancing of risks, often is worse than no regulation at all."[3] I have yet to talk to an investor who thinks more regulation would be good for the industry. Self-regulation is far better than government regulation, and Wall Street is not alone in waking up to this fact. Main Street also prefers self-regulation to government regulation, which explains why 78 percent of companies in general have boards of directors that set ethical standards, up from 41 percent in 1991 and 21 percent in 1987. Again, the *Wall Street Journal* summed up the situation well: "business leaders see . . . self-regulation as a way to avoid legislative or judicial intrusions."[4]

Another compelling reason to focus on ethics is client concern. The public sees investment professionals as less ethical than lawyers and doctors. Only politicians rate worse than investment professionals. **Figure 1** shows that more than 35 percent of respondents cited ethics as the most important issue in the

---

[1] Formerly called Jim Ware & Associates.

[2] "Wall Street Rules," *Wall Street Journal* (August 8, 1999):A18.

[3] "Mad Regulatory Disease," *Wall Street Journal* (August 24, 1999):A16.

[4] *Wall Street Journal* (September 3, 1999):A1.

profession. And when it comes to hiring criteria for investment professionals, individual investors ranked ethics ahead of fees and style. Considering the importance that investors place on ethics, ethics may be underutilized in investment marketing.

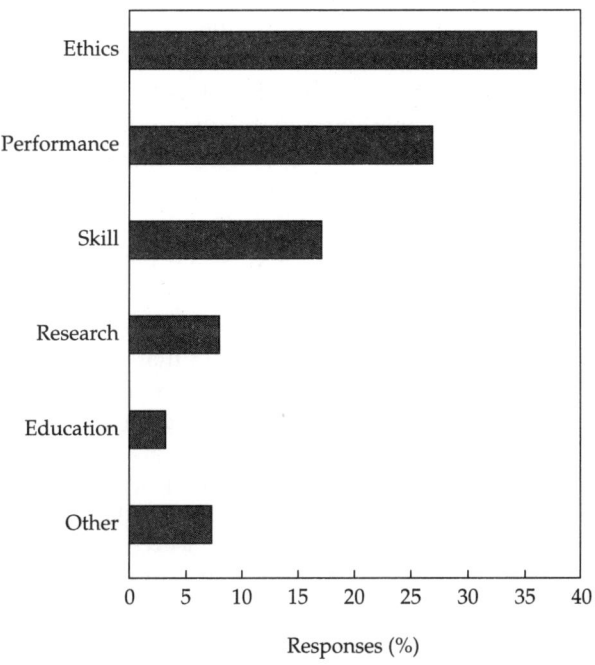

Figure 1. Survey Responses Indicating the Most Important Issue in the Investment Profession

Source: Based on data from R. Edward Freeman's presentation, "Ethics in the Investment Management Profession," 1999 AIMR Annual Conference, Orlando, FL.

Definitions of Ethical

To sort out the gray area, some definitions of what it means to be ethical might be helpful. Ernest Hemingway said, "What is ethical is what you feel good after, and what is unethical is what you feel bad after." Is that true? I see people on the highway driving on the shoulder so that they can get ahead of the other cars (i.e., cutting in line), and they seem to feel great about it. But most of us would agree that cutting in line is unethical.

Thomas Jefferson argued that an ethical person "observes those moral precepts in which all religions concur." Follow the Golden Rule: Treat others as you would like to be treated. Some people argue that a fiduciary relationship means that the fiduciary must follow the Golden Rule, but Albert Carr, in an article in the *Harvard Business Review*, writes that business-people must do away with the Golden Rule. He argues that "The ethics of business are not those of society, but rather those of the poker game." Warren Buffett compares investing with poker and writes, "If after ten minutes of playing poker, you can't figure out who the patsy is . . . it's YOU!" Good poker players are praised for their skill at bluffing. Similarly, good boxers win by faking punches and then delivering unexpected real ones. Good business executives do the same. They must know when to bluff and when to deliver knockout blows. George Bernard Shaw said, "It is always the best policy to speak the truth, unless, of course, you are an exceptionally good liar!" Shaw was also praising the art of bluffing.

The implication is that being good at investing requires using Golden Gloves, not the Golden Rule. Investment managers seemingly have to choose between being (1) ethical and broke or (2) sleazy and loaded. Business examples support this either/or view. Recently, Microsoft Corporation was voted the top company in technology on a financial basis, but it was very low on the "warm-fuzzy-place-to-work" scale.

Ethics in Investment Management

Using Golden Gloves and the Golden Rule in investing is not an either/or construct but, rather, a both/and construct. Golden Gloves and the Golden Rule are necessary and useful, but in different settings. I call them "tough" and "tender" ethics. The Golden Glove ethics are tough; the Golden Rule ethics are tender. Tender ethics are necessary and useful in fiduciary relationships in which the client's interests come first. Tough ethics are necessary in the capital markets where "perform or die" is the rule. Those who use tough ethics seek win/lose situations; those who use tender ethics seek win/win situations. The main fear of the tough-ethics people is being incompetent; the main fear of the tender-ethics people is being uncompassionate.

Sadly, the either/or thinking on both sides results in efforts to crush the opponent, rather than recognizing and leveraging the strength of each position. In investing, the truly excellent firms should develop skills in both tough and tender ethics.

Many of the issues in the gray area are caused by the collision of tough and tender, and the only way around these difficulties is clarity. The key questions are (1) what are the rules and (2) can we agree to them. Investing is a relationship business. The single biggest danger in all relationships is assumptions. Three rules keep people out of ethical trouble in relationships: clarify, clarify, clarify. Do not assume, ask.

Tough Ethics. Where are tough ethics useful? What role do they play? Where do they cause problems? Tough ethics are useful in competitive situations in which the players know the rules and can take care of themselves.

A recent event in the world of professional football illustrates a point about tough ethics. The National Football League (NFL) is fiercely competitive. All conventions of civilized behavior are abandoned, and violence rules. Professional football is a huge business ($17 billion), and fans love it. The way that players battle one another on the field would be criminal outside the stadium. Players are encouraged to be aggressive and intimidating on the field. Frequently, they go too far, and flags are thrown for "unnecessary roughness." A penalty is assessed, and the game goes on. Occasionally, however, a major violation occurs, such as when Mark Carrier of the Detroit Lions delivered a bone-crushing, helmet-to-helmet blow that knocked the other player unconscious. Carrier was fined $50,000 and suspended.

Was Carrier's hit unethical? Interestingly, Tom Waddle, an ex-NFL player, said:

> I think that the penalty was way too severe. Sad thing is, Mark's not a dirty player. Mark is playing the game the way that he has always known how to play it. The last thing that I would have done would be to whine about how hard a guy hit me, with his helmet or without. I don't think the players have as much of an issue with it as the league does.[5]

Although the action was judged illegal and resulted in a fine and suspension, few players or media people saw Carrier's action as unethical—illegal but not unethical.

Consider, then, this example about investing in *Street Smarts: Linking Professional Conduct with Shareholder Value in the Securities Industry*:

> In one 1995 case reported in *Business Week*, an investor entrusted her nest egg of $800,000 to Shearson Lehman for investment in common stock. Her broker made $100,000 of stock purchases against her wishes and undertook large trades on margin in order to generate margin-interest income ($18,124) and commission income ($20,134). The net profit to her was $2,158. The investor then shifted her account to another firm, a discount house. Her broker at that firm also churned her account, this time in OTC stocks. She pulled her account, but the same thing happened at a third and fourth firm. In the end, her stake had shriveled to $370,000. The customer in this case blames herself for her own naivete. But the question remains: Is there any other industry in which a customer needs to worry about getting taken to the cleaners by four successive vendors?[6]

In contrast to the football example, none of the advisors were fined or suspended. No legal action was taken. But most people would judge those actions as highly unethical, even reprehensible. The situation is funny only in *A Midsummer Night's Sex Comedy*, when Woody Allen, playing an investment advisor, said, "My style is to invest people's money until there is nothing left."

What is the difference between the football and the broker example? Why is one illegal yet ethical and the other legal but unethical? The answer lies in the tough/tender distinction. NFL players understand that they are playing by tough ethics each time they suit up for a game. They are highly trained experts who are paid a great sum of money for the poundings they endure. Likewise, professional investors know and accept the risks they face when battling other professionals.

In fact, the U.S. SEC's Mary Podesta supported this "fair fight" view when she said that:

> institutional or large clients of money managers can be expected to fend for themselves and that all of the requirements that apply to investment advisors in their dealings with clients perhaps need not apply to large accounts. . . . Our real concern is with the advertising practices and the other standards that apply when advisors are dealing with the general public.[7]

If Salomon Smith Barney beats up on Goldman, Sachs & Company, Mike Wallace will not show up at their offices with a camera crew.

When professionals battle one another, on the football field or in the trading room, the question of ethics almost disappears. Legalities still remain, and overly aggressive participants do step over the line and get penalized. But few participants are likely to complain that they were treated unethically. Why? Because the contestants are competing against equals who know the rules and the risks. It is a fair fight, a level playing field. Some teams or firms will develop reputations for being "dirty," which will require the opponents to devise compensating strategies: A lineman in the NFL makes remarks about an opposing player's mother's footwear, and that player learns to ignore it; a pension fund manager gives performance

---

[5] *Chicago Tribune* (October 14, 1999):Sports section.

[6] Roy C. Smith and Ingo Walter, *Street Smarts: Linking Professional Conduct with Shareholder Value in the Securities Industry* (Watertown, MA: Harvard Business School Press, 1997):73.

[7] Mary Podesta, "Where the SEC Stands on Performance Advertising and Other Issues," in *Performance Reporting for Investment Managers: Applying the AIMR Performance Presentation Standards* (Charlottesville, VA: AIMR, 1990):23.

numbers that are not adjusted for risk, and the client adjusts them.

The key attributes, then, of both NFL players and professional investors are that (1) they are tough-minded competitors who enjoy winning a good fight and (2) they are armed with the knowledge and skills to compete effectively. These attributes can be arranged in a grid, with ethical stance along one side and knowledge level along the other, as shown in **Exhibit 1**. The investors who belong "on the playing field" believe in tough ethics and are highly knowledgeable. No one else belongs on the field. Likewise, the "on-field" behavior must not leave the "stadium." Investment professionals who use tough ethics with a novice investor run the risk of exploiting the investor's ignorance and trust.

Exhibit 1. Golden Gloves versus the Golden Rule

		Knowledge Level	
		Novice	Expert
Ethical Stance	Tough	Exploit Ignorance	Fair Fight
	Tender	Exploit Ignorance and Trust	Exploit Trust

Tender Ethics. Tender ethics are most appropriately used with the novice investor. AIMR says that investment professionals "are in a position to exploit their customers' trust and ignorance, and therefore, they are held to a higher duty of care."[8] More than 90 percent of investment professionals are located in the "fair fight" box and have been trained to operate in that manner. But investing is a fiduciary business, which means having a special relationship of trust with the client. Much of the general public does not know common stock from livestock. A recent survey showed that 15 percent of respondents did not know that they could lose money in the stock market. Adopting a "buyer beware" attitude with such investors would be unethical and unsporting. The SEC and AIMR are very clear about what fiduciary means: Client interests must come first. The Golden Rule (tender ethics) should reign.

The tender/tough and novice/expert distinctions illuminate the gray areas in ethics. They help identify how the client is at a disadvantage. The question is: Will managers look for creative ways to add value for clients, or will they use their creativity to pull the wool over clients' eyes?

Examples of Gray Area

All of the following examples illustrate ethical dilemmas for active investment managers.

Overconfidence. All human beings are guilty of thinking they know a little bit more than they do. Analysts (and their estimates) are no exception. Therefore, is it ethical for online trading companies to encourage amateurs to think that they are professionals? One such ad shows a bearded, wise elder saying, "It's me versus 9,734 stocks. I like my odds." Another shows a young woman beaming with confidence as she says, "I don't want to just beat the market. I want to wrestle its scrawny little body to the ground and make it beg for mercy." Is this advice in the best interests of clients?

Hot-Hand Advertising. Marketers are aware that the general public typically believes in the "hot-hand" phenomenon: A basketball player who has sunk five shots in a row has a hot hand and is more likely to make the sixth attempt; a fund manager who has had a hot year is believed to be on a roll. Studies have disproved the hot-hand theory, but it is nevertheless seductive. And despite clear guidelines to the contrary from AIMR and the SEC, investment firms continue to advertise one-year results. (AIMR recommends that firms provide 10 years of historical performance and an appropriate benchmark; the SEC is clear in its statement about advertising: "Advisors are responsible for ensuring that their performance materials are not deceptive or misleading."[9]) One recent ad proclaimed "Avoid the rush. Retire early" and then showed a one-year return of 45.9 percent versus 1.5 percent for the Russell 2000 Index. Dean LeBaron, who helped devise the AIMR Performance Presentation Standards, stated that they could have included a range of significance to the numbers but that doing so would have shown that most have no meaning.

Relative Performance. Investing is a relative game, a fact that experts know but the general public often does not. Many mutual fund ads provide 10-year numbers and more stars (from the rating agencies) than on Academy Awards night. But these same ads do not provide relevant benchmarks or risk adjustments. One such ad recently appeared next to the Performance Benchmarks section in the *Wall*

---

[8] Association for Investment Management and Research, *Standards of Practice Handbook*, 7th ed. (Charlottesville, VA: AIMR, 1996):163.

[9] Podesta, "Where the SEC Stands on Performance Advertising and Other Issues":22.

Street Journal. The ad highlighted the firm's growth and income fund's five-year record: 15.76 percent. By most standards, this number is impressive—much better than certificates of deposit or money market funds. But the benchmark section right next to this ad showed that the average growth and income fund returned 21.81 percent over the same five-year period. Furthermore, the S&P 500 Index returned 27.14 percent, presumably with less turnover and less risk. Again, is this sort of advertising in the best interests of clients?

Advertising Fees. Is it ethical for mutual funds to charge advertising fees? Nearly 7,000 of the 13,000 mutual funds do. One recent study of front-end loads and 12b-1 fees, however, showed that "marketing charges do not add any real value to the financial performance of mutual funds."[10] In his most recent book, John Bogle cites a Harvard Business School doctoral paper that came to a similar conclusion: "There is no evidence that 12b-1 fees generate benefits which are passed along to fund shareholders who pay these fees."[11] Is charging such fees pulling a fast one on the public, similar to when cigarette companies advertised that smoking was *good* for your health? Will the surgeon general of investing, SEC Chair Arthur Levitt, have to package funds with a warning label: Caution, advertising fees are hazardous to your financial health?

Fund Size. Is it in clients' best interest for fund managers to chant the popular mantra: Grow big grow fast, grow big grow fast. Surely, growth does result in some economies of scale, but at what point are they outweighed by factors such as higher transaction costs? Some researchers have found that "As assets under management increase, so do the block sizes of the firm's trades. The resulting higher transaction costs have a negative impact on performance."[12] Langdon Wheeler has said that his company, Numeric Investors, "measures success by the dollars of excess return generated for the clients rather than dollars of assets under management. We focus on returns, not marketing."[13]

Research. Whose interests are being served when investment firms censor their analysts? Such was the case with banking analyst Sean Ryan at Bear Stearns; his supervisors told him not to make negative comments about First Union. Commenting on this situation and others like it, Siva Nathan, an accounting professor at Georgia State University, said, "This is the reason why sell-side analysts are losing their credibility."[14] Is it in clients' best interest to limit analysts' ability to report on their research?

Broker Compensation. Brokers have a fiduciary responsibility to their clients, and yet the huge, up-front pay packages that many brokers are receiving may, according to Arthur Levitt, "motivate brokers to encourage transactions that aren't in the clients' best interest."[15] The result is that more regulation is likely: mandatory disclosure when brokers ask their customers to transfer their accounts to a firm that has paid the broker to ask for the switch.

Passive Active Funds. Joel Dickson, a principal at the Vanguard Group, said, "I chuckle every time I see a new tax-managed fund that comes out and says, 'we're going to employ a low turnover, buy-and-hold strategy.' Why would I pay an active-management price for an index fund?"[16] Is it in clients' best interest to charge active management fees for passive management?

Regulation

The formula for successful self-regulation starts with a healthy respect for the opponents—greed and self-interest—and a long-term commitment to battle them one day at a time. No quick fixes or shortcuts exist. And measurement is critical. Firms get what they measure. If firms measure only production and profits, then that is what they will get, by any means necessary. Education and assessment are imperative, and they pay off, as one company—Lockheed Martin Corporation—is showing with its step-by-step, computerized training on ethics and legal compliance. **Table 1** shows the significant improvement over the past five years as a result of its program.

Conversely, the formula for more government regulation is to ignore the problem and hope that it will magically go away.

---

[10] John Kihn, "To Load or Not to Load? A Study of the Marketing and Distribution Charges of Mutual Funds," *Financial Analysts Journal* (May/June 1996):35.

[11] John C. Bogle, *Common Sense on Mutual Funds: New Imperatives for the Intelligent Investor* (New York: John Wiley & Sons, 1999):339.

[12] Philip Halpern, Nancy Calkins, and Tom Ruggels, "Does the Emperor Wear Clothes or Not? The Final Word (or Almost) on the Parable of Investment Management," *Financial Analysts Journal* (July/August 1996):14.

[13] Langdon B. Wheeler, "The Value of Added Value: The Smaller Active Manager's Approach to the Future," in *The Future of Investment Management* (Charlottesville, VA: AIMR, 1998):49.

[14] Rick Brooks, "Heard on the Street: Speak No Evil? Analysts Turn Silent on Bank," *Wall Street Journal* (August 17, 1999):C1.

[15] Randall Smith, "Wall Street Still Spends Big to Court Top Brokers," *Wall Street Journal* (July 14, 1999):C1.

[16] Bill Barnhart, "Manager's Task Is to Minimize Taxable Income," *Chicago Tribune* (October 2, 1999).

Table 1. Results of Lockheed Martin's Ethics and Compliance Program (number of incidents)

Sanction	1995	1999
Discharge	56	25
Suspension	47	14
Written reprimand	59	51
Oral reprimand	164	146
Other	60	66
Total sanctions	386	302

Summary

Investing, by its very nature, implies that one person is trying to get the better of another. For investors to make money, one person must buy (sell) to the disadvantage of another. But as long as it is a "fair fight," most people do not consider investing to be unethical. When ethics do come into play is when it is not a fair fight—when one person has an edge over another and purposely exploits that edge.

Unfortunately, in the investment industry, the potential exists for clients to be disadvantaged compared with their money managers, because of either clients' attitudes (tender) or knowledge (novice) about investing or both, hence the need for a fiduciary relationship in which clients' needs are placed first. When money managers take a "buyer beware" approach with clients, they are committing an ethical breach. And the larger the disparity in attitude and knowledge between manager and client, the more reprehensible the misconduct. And the more frequent and reprehensible the conduct is in the industry, the more likely it is that the government will step in and impose regulations. Wise investment professionals, for the sake of the industry, will support AIMR in its goal of "setting a higher standard" and enforcing it.

Question and Answer Session

James W. Ware, CFA

Question: Why is more regulation so horrible?

Ware: In theory, regulation could be fine because you could get intelligent people saying this is what is wrong and we'll take over for AIMR and help out and do the things that need to be done in the industry. In practice, regulation never quite seems to work the way it is supposed to work; it always creates inefficiencies and more cost.

Question: What is your opinion about the widespread use of defined-contribution plans when we know most investors know very little about investing?

Ware: In my last assignment, I went around the country talking to employees of a Fortune 500 company about their investment options. It was a little like having the Perrier concession in the Sahara. Employees mobbed me after my talk to get input about their portfolios. The main investment issue was asset allocation. Given the youthfulness of these employees, most of them had way too much invested in low risk/low return assets. Is it unethical? I don't think so; the intention is not to "pull one over" on the employees. Rather, they are being empowered to manage their own financial affairs. Do some employees make poor decisions? Absolutely. But that's different from the employer trying to hoodwink them.

Question: With all the press and educational materials aimed at investors, do you think investors are becoming more sophisticated?

Ware: Certainly. The Terminex guy who sprays my house for bugs gives me lectures about inflation, money supply, and foreign exchange rates that would impress Abby Cohen. I think the wall has collapsed between professional investors and amateurs. What used to be considered a technical, arcane subject is now seen as a relatively straightforward enterprise, thanks to Peter Lynch and others who have a gift for clarity and simplicity. The danger is that people will get cocky and stray from sound investing, the kind that John Bogle describes: long term, low fees, low turnover, good diversification.

Question: Is it ethical to have a dual standard saying that the same rules do not apply when two investment professionals are conducting business and when a professional and nonprofessional are?

Ware: Good question. Dual standards exist in all walks of life. The key is what accounts for the two standards. For example, an insurance company quotes a different rate to a man and woman with the same age and geographic location. We don't consider that unethical.

The core of the issue is the fiduciary responsibility of the professional investor. She is required to put her client's financial matters ahead of her self-interest. A bond trader at Goldman Sachs, however, is not asked to do this when he battles a Salomon trader for the best deal. As competitors, they are encouraged to "get the better" of the other. And that's really the essence of my talk, the difference between competition and cooperation: Golden Gloves and the Golden Rule.

Question: Who would you say are the ethical role models in the industry?

Ware: I'm sure that thousands of money managers are doing a wonderfully competent job. They're the ones who faithfully do their duties and fill out the AIMR compliance card each year. We just don't hear about them. Of the more celebrated investors, I think that Warren Buffett and John Bogle take their ethical responsibilities seriously. Ironically, Mike Milken may have become a role model, showing once again how things are always changing.

Corporate Conduct and Professional Integrity: A Survey

Andrew E. Nolan
*Managing Partner, Regulatory Compliance Consulting Group
PricewaterhouseCoopers LLP*

> Ethical practices are considered crucial by most investment professionals, but survey results show that the implementation and awareness of ethical policies vary among firms. Survey respondents also commented on what they perceive to be the hot risk topics, such as insider trading, in the industry. Finally, by not publicizing their attitude toward ethics and compliance and by not issuing reports of the risk controls in place, firms may be missing an opportunity to gain competitive advantage.

Put your clients before yourself; that statement is the heart of ethics in investment management. So, about a year ago, several of us in Pricewaterhouse-Coopers' Regulatory Compliance Consulting Group came up with the idea of doing a survey to see how people perceive ethics and compliance in the investment management industry. Our goal was to measure industry concerns surrounding business ethics and professional conduct and to get information regarding the type and nature of programs designed to address ethics and professional conduct and compliance. The results show that industry leaders pay a great deal of attention to matters of ethics and professional integrity and that the vast majority of investment management firms have well-developed compliance programs to address ethics and professional conduct. The details follow.

Survey Data

We surveyed 65 U.S.-based firms in the investment management industry. The results were published April 15, 1999. Responding firms ranged from local niche shops to large multinational investment complexes. More than 20 of the responding firms had assets greater than $50 billion. In total, the respondents represented assets under management in excess of $1 trillion.

Most firms responding (73 percent) were subsidiaries of a larger financial institution; 34 percent had insurance companies as parent companies, 17 percent had banks as parents, 6 percent had broker/dealers as parents, and 35 percent listed other. That 35 percent is the asset management operations of what people normally think of as smokestack companies.

The people responding were the more senior people in the organization. Only 3 percent of respondents listed themselves as managers; the rest listed themselves as vice president/officer or higher. They also reflected a wealth of experience; 57 percent were in the business for 10–20 years, and 23 percent had more than 20 years of experience, for a total of about 80 percent with more than 10 years of experience in the industry.

Program Goals, Design, and Implementation

Compliance programs are designed to address directly three areas—fiduciary responsibility, regulatory and corporate compliance, and personal conduct of employees—and indirectly the reputation of the firm.

Interestingly, the firms surveyed did not seem to take advantage of, or market themselves on the basis of, having sound policies and procedures for compliance and ethics. Only 20 percent of the respondents said they publish ethics-related efforts in reports to shareholders and clients, and just 30 percent said they highlight ethics programs in marketing brochures, which is interesting considering that 89 percent of the firms viewed reputation management and enhancement as an important by-product of sound corporate compliance policies and procedures, as shown in **Table 1**. Our conclusion from these findings is that,

©2000, Association for Investment Management and Research

Table 1. Perceived Benefits of Ethics Programs

Benefit	Percentage of Respondents
Protects reputation	89%
Educates employees about appropriate conduct	89
Improves risk management	78
Protects assets	72
Minimizes risk of adverse publicity	70
Reduces potential costs	58
Eliminates ambiguity about remediation	39
Aids in marketing services	34

Note: Results do not equal 100 percent because some respondents selected more than one answer.

---

at present, firms may be missing an opportunity to gain competitive advantage by "wearing on their sleeves" their attitude toward ethics and compliance.

The design and implementation of a compliance program varied considerably from one organization to the next. This finding is not surprising because ethics is very subjective, and a compliance program must meet the needs of the given organization, be it centralized or decentralized, large or small, and so on. Large firms, however, tended to have more formal programs than small firms. The variation among firms seems to exist mainly with respect to the internal communication of ethics programs, awareness measurement (i.e., testing employees to see if they understand what their responsibilities are regarding compliance and ethical behavior), and enforcement, which consists of two pieces: remediation and retribution. Remediation refers to making clients whole, doing the right thing with respect to an affected party externally, and retribution refers to what steps are taken internally with respect to someone who violates the compliance program or the code of ethics.

Fewer than 10 percent of the respondents reported that ethics is incorporated in their mission statement. Only slightly more than 10 percent actually had an ethics committee to focus on policies and procedures and to deal with ethical issues that came up, and only 30 percent indicated that ethics policies were included in procedure manuals. Furthermore, 50 percent of the respondents indicated that they did not have an assessment plan in place by which managers could determine whether the employees responsible for complying with the code of ethics actually understood it. Out of the large firms (those with more than $50 billion in assets under management), two-thirds had some way of testing to make sure that the employees, the money managers, understood and complied with their ethical responsibilities under the code of conduct of the firm. Our conclusion from these findings is that more could be done to improve ethics awareness by proactive communication with the people in the firm who are responsible for complying.

Perhaps one of the most interesting findings that came out of this survey has to do with how firms become aware of policy infringements. The good news is that 81 percent of the respondents said that they became aware of violations either through their own compliance or legal department or internal audit examinations, as shown in **Table 2**, and 78 percent cited compliance tracking reports, which is also encouraging because it shows that a system is in place to track compliance. The interesting finding is that the third and fourth most frequently cited sources were customer complaints and regulatory inspections. Naturally, a firm will learn about compliance or ethical violations from clients or regulators, but learning about infractions this way is obviously less than ideal.

Table 2. How Firms Are Made Aware of Policy Infringements

Method	Percentage of Respondents
Compliance/legal department or internal audit	81%
Compliance tracking reports	78
Regulatory inspection	44
Client complaint	28
External audit examinations	23
Employee hotline/ombudsman	14
Anonymous call/letter	14
Ethics office	11
Other	5

Note: Results do not equal 100 percent because some respondents selected more than one answer.

Sixty-five percent of respondents indicated that they performed a periodic review of their compliance programs, but a contradiction exists as to how and when the programs were reviewed. Keep in mind that respondents indicated that among the ways infringements were identified were regulatory exams and customer complaints, although the vast majority of compliance problems were found through internal controls. If a money management firm finds that it is learning of regulatory compliance violations, violations of the code of conduct, and so on more from external sources than internal sources, then the firm should consider whether it has adequate controls in place, because those kinds of surprises from external sources should not occur.

Also, 28 percent of the respondents said they do not have a formal remediation or retribution policy, and 16 percent said they were not sure. With respect to retribution, firms should have a formalized policy whereby employees understand the consequences if they violate the code of conduct. The case for having a formalized remediation policy (i.e., keeping the customer whole for whatever affected the customer's investment) is not as clear. The problem is that a firm can have a policy in place, but if an important enough customer comes and makes a demand of the firm, even though the firm does not think it was wrong, the firm will probably pay up if the profit equation is right. So, remediation policies tend to be very *ad hoc*, which is true not only for investment management firms but also for custodians, transfer agents, and most service organizations in the investment management business.

For remediation and retribution policies, only 6 percent of respondents had a highly structured policy and 30 percent moderately structured; 20 percent exclusively used a case-by-case approach. If I could do the survey again, I would ask about the remediation and retribution policies separately because I think retribution tends to be more structured than remediation, and asking questions about the two together probably skewed the data. When we asked who is typically responsible for remediation and retribution policies and the determination of those policies, respondents listed compliance officer, executive review committee, and general counsel (in that order).

Risk Topics

The survey asked respondents to comment on what they saw as the hot risk topics—areas of concern in the investment management industry today. For example, we asked if insider trading was an area of concern; it was across the board. Although respondents said insider trading was an area of high concern, it would not necessarily keep the CEO of a money management firm awake at night because firms typically have very good controls over insider trading. Thus, even though insider trading is an area of concern in the industry, it is not a big problem because controls are in place to make sure that problems do not occur. Personal trading was cited as an industrywide concern. Advertising of performance information, trade allocations, initial public offering (IPO) allocations, and the use (or maybe the misuse) of derivatives were all highlighted as areas of general concern. Furthermore, respondents said that having professional accreditations, such as a CFA charter, indicates a high level of professional conduct and a high level of professional ethics.

Reporting Controls

Money management firms are increasingly focusing on controls. The AICPA (American Institute of Certified Public Accountants), through its Statement of Auditing Standards #70, allows a firm to report to the world about the controls it has in place. In the case of a money management firm, it can report on the controls over the management of money. In the past in the investment management industry, reports on controls tended to focus on custodians and transfer agents. Nobody thought of a money manager as a service organization to investors, particularly institutional investors, but institutional investors are starting to see money managers in this light. Institutional investors are realizing that the risk in their portfolios is composed of market risk and operating risk and that the operating risk associated with a custodian or a transfer agent is probably a lot less than the risk inherent in the management of their money. For example, investors are exposed to the risk that a money manager does not comply with the investment guidelines or the trading desk does not allocate trades properly among portfolios. So, a lot of institutional investors are asking for reports on controls from investment managers. My understanding is that a couple of the largest institutional investors are requiring some sort of report on controls before they give investment mandates. Right now, firms that can produce such a report can gain a competitive advantage. In three or four years, having such a report will be absolutely necessary.

A report on risk controls for money managers typically covers four areas. The first area is portfolio management, which has to do with compliance with investment guidelines and investment restrictions. Some people even go into commentaries about due diligence on investment research. The second area is trade allocation. The third area is the accuracy of reports to the clients; that is, how do clients know that what gets spit out of the computer is accurate in terms of position, performance, and so on. The fourth area is the computer controls underlying all of those functions.

Question and Answer Session

Andrew E. Nolan

Question: Did any of the survey results surprise you?

Nolan: The biggest surprise was the fact that so many respondents considered external sources (regulatory examinations or customer complaints) to be one of the ways they find out about compliance violations. Another surprise was that firms don't make more of their ethics and compliance programs in their marketing efforts, particularly because institutional investors are paying increasing attention to who they are doing business with and what controls are in place.

Some other findings were fairly intuitive, such as the larger the organization, the more formalized the programs and procedures. Probably a lot of the small, niche shops that filled out the survey are wondering if they have the infrastructure necessary to meet their compliance needs.

Question: Did you discover anything interesting about trade allocation?

Nolan: We didn't ask much about the trade allocation process. We just asked if trade allocation was an area of concern, and the answer was yes.

In practice, some of the concerns are favorable allocations and late allocations. For example, a lot of firms use the average price at which they execute the order during the course of the day. But if somebody comes in at 4:00 p.m., should that person get the average price or is there a time when you say the investor is not getting the average but an actual for that transaction? So, there are a lot of issues in trade allocations.

The whole question of best execution is one of the hardest ones to deal with in the investment management industry because so many intangibles, such as soft dollars, go into it. How do you put all those intangibles into something that is a quantifiable, objective determination of best execution? I don't know whether the U.S. SEC is going to let soft dollars survive much longer because without soft dollars, it is a lot easier to determine what the execution is and whether you are getting best execution.

Question: For many years, the sell side of the industry has received greater scrutiny by regulatory agencies than the buy side. Do you think that this scrutiny is likely to turn toward the buy side?

Nolan: I think the SEC does concentrate on the buy side. In theory, the SEC should visit every manager once every three years. The SEC's emphasis continues to be on the sell side to make sure that people understand what they're getting into, particularly with insurance distribution channels—where they are distributing mutual funds to insurance carriers and thousands of independent agents are out there selling mutual funds. But the SEC does look at the manufacturing side, the buy side, and goes into the actual investment decision-making process, trade execution, and so on. I think the buy side has always been an area of focus.

Question: What is Rule 17j-1 and what are the recent modifications?

Nolan: Rule 17j-1 of the Investment Company Act of 1940 addresses the code of ethics for mutual funds and personal securities trading by mutual fund personnel. In the fall of 1999, the SEC adopted amendments to Rule 17j-1 that tightened the regulation of mutual fund managers and their investment advisors who trade for their own accounts. Specifically, the amendments require that "access persons" report their holdings initially and on an annual basis. In addition, the amendments require access persons to get approval prior to purchasing an IPO or a private placement. Another significant change is that the amendments require that the directors of a mutual fund approve the code of ethics of the mutual fund and those of its investment advisors.

Measuring, Controlling, and Allocating Trading Costs

Wayne H. Wagner
Chairman
Plexus Group

> Total trading costs include more than just the commission, which is the tip of the iceberg of trading costs. Only by looking at the total trading costs can money managers assess whether a trade adds or subtracts value from a portfolio. Consequently, managers need to know how to measure trading costs and how to quantify best execution. In addition, managers need to be able to determine whether directed trades can be used effectively and, ultimately, in a client's best interests.

Metaphorically speaking, a portfolio's assets are locked in a safe, and dipping into them is very difficult. But when assets are being moved from one place to another (as they are during trading), they take on liquid-like qualities, and that "liquid" can splash out of the appropriate containers. Consequently, transaction costs and best execution have become hot topics in regulatory circles. Furthermore, sensitivity to cost is as effective a way of attaining competitive performance as having superior investment insights. Otherwise, the index fund, which has no insight at all, would not be competitive on a performance basis, and of course, it is.

Combining active management with effective cost control comes to many investment managers as a strange idea. A manager once told me, "I pick stocks. The rest is just plumbing." I could not convince that manager that leaky plumbing does not maximize the value of a house. Most investment managers think that if they have bad performance, then either they need better investment ideas or better traders who are able to get the good investment ideas into the portfolios.

In this presentation, I begin by providing a brief background on trading costs and commissions. Next, I describe the measurement methods available for benchmarking trading costs and show the results of our analysis at the Plexus Group. I will go into some depth on the value (or lack thereof) of using commission recapture, and finally, I will cover some of the major trading issues from a cost perspective.

Background

The industry grew up by making its money on the transaction fee (instead of the management of the assets) and by encouraging managers, brokers, and so on to trade those assets rather than to hold them, irrespective of what seemed to be in the best interest of the investor (whether individual, corporate, or mutual fund investor). As a result, analyzing and focusing on transaction costs sometimes meets with resistance.

Originally, commissions were set by the exchanges. On May 1, 1975, commissions became negotiable. When commissions became negotiable, numerous opportunities opened up. Investors could suddenly shop around for the lowest commission, or by using directed commissions, they could buy services from outside providers.

In the 1980s, the U.S. Department of Labor announced that it considered commissions to be plan assets and, as such, requiring fiduciary oversight. Therefore, commissions must be managed as though they are fund assets. Meanwhile, the functional, economic definition of trading costs was expanded to include both commissions and market impact.

In the 1990s, people began to look at total implementation costs, which include opportunity and delay costs as well as commissions and impact. The U.S. SEC also started to become much more aggressive about monitoring manager compliance and control.

Measurement Methods

Trading is anti-performance. Any money that goes out of the portfolio as a trading expense is no longer in the portfolio to continue compounding. Measured in dollar-weighted returns, anything that flows out of the fund never to come back in is an impediment to future returns and certainly an impediment to funding retirement, which is the reason why most investment managers have assets to manage. These frictional costs for moving assets around are real, and they affect performance. But no one knows how big these frictional costs are supposed to be. Is 25 basis points (bps) good? Is 100 bps good? Is 200 bps good? How much transaction cost is necessary to run the process so that the investment ideas can flow into the portfolio and the value of those investment ideas can benefit the portfolio? Essentially, investment advisors must determine whether trading adds value or detracts value for clients, recognizing that some trading costs are necessary.

To find out whether a trade is value enhancing or value detracting, trading costs can be benchmarked in several ways, and the overall impact of a trade can also be quantified.

Daily-Average Method. One way to benchmark trading costs is to use the daily volume-weighted average price, or a similar daily-average measure. The problem is deciding what is good and what is bad. Consider the following sequence: Bad news comes out on a stock late in the day, and the portfolio manager tells the trader to sell whatever she can. She gets a big trade off near the market close at the worst price of the day. When looking at the daily average, the trade appears to be a bad one. But what if the impact of that news had not yet filtered completely through the marketplace, and the next day, the stock drops 5 percent? From this next-day perspective, the trade looks like a pretty good one. In the right context, the trade is seen as capturing value as efficiently as possible.

Similar-Trade Comparison. Another way to benchmark costs is to use a similar-trade comparison. The question is what did other people executing similar trades pay to execute those trades. By similar, what is meant are trades with similar characteristics made in similar market conditions. Trading 50 percent of a day's volume is obviously more expensive than trading 5 percent of a day's volume. Typically, trading in a $1 billion company is more expensive than trading in a $100 billion company. Furthermore, trading in the absence of company news is a lot easier and cheaper than when news is out. That is, trading can become quite difficult in momentum conditions caused by news, changed recommendations, or new data. Many traders will then compete to be the one to win the prize of securing liquidity to actualize a manager's investment ideas.

Cost of Capture Model. If a portfolio has X dollars before going into the transaction and Y dollars after, the cost to execute that transaction is $X - Y$. Consider a plan sponsor that has terminated a manager and decides to liquidate the portfolio using an agency program. If the plan sponsor started with $100 million and ended up with $98 million, $2 million was the cost of going from a portfolio of stocks to a portfolio of cash.

For individual trades, the concept is similarly applied, but applying this approach has been difficult because nobody knows exactly how to specify the initial value of X in the equation. The question often arises as to what was the defining event that started this trading activity. If people looked at only what was being executed, they would miss the true cost details involved in the timing of the trade. If a trade was on the trading desk on Monday but did not get executed until Tuesday, the difference in price movement between Monday and Tuesday would need to be accounted for. That is, information is needed about who said what and when (i.e., when did the portfolio manager create something actionable on his own trade desk—not when it was shown to a broker).

The nice thing about this cost of capture model is that it shows the commission in proper context. A manager who decides to reduce commissions might be forgoing some needed broker skills. The actual costs may have gone into impact or into delay, and this model will allow the manager to see them. A trader who is evaluated or compensated based on beating the volume-weighted average price can hold the order over to the next day, thus getting a crack at a new volume-weighted average price that may be easier to best. The manager, please note, does not get a new strike price. Consequently, value and performance are lost.

The trader frequently becomes the scapegoat for bad performance. As consultants, we like to think that we are hired to help people perform better and to improve the performance of funds. I fear that all too often we are hired to fire the trader because nobody wants to do it. Imagine a portfolio manager's surprise when we tell her that the problem is that she has been dribbling these orders out while the price has been moving away. We are often the trader's best friend because of the comprehensive view that we give of the quality of the execution being provided (if there is quality execution).

Our data at the Plexus Group show that the average institutional dollar traded is traded as a portion of an order that exceeds a day's trading volume. The growth in assets that has been confounding portfolio managers results in rapidly growing trade size.

As much as market liquidity has expanded, the need for liquidity is even greater because managers have increasingly notched up the average size of a trade, measured in terms of the percentage of the daily volume.

If a trader had an order to buy 500,000 shares and took seven days to complete that trade because the stock was trading an average of 100,000 shares a day (and he did not want to dominate that trading pattern), delay costs should be expected. Delays can result from the size of the order or because the portfolio manager dribbles the order out to the trader in pieces. Or maybe the trader cannot find the other side of the trade. Why the delay occurred shows up in the interpretation of the data, not in the data themselves.

Note that a trader cannot trade without finding somebody who thinks the opposite of what she (or her portfolio manager) is thinking. The trader bets that her (or the portfolio manager's) information sources are better than those of the person who is selling the stock. This process is quite different from that of the portfolio manager, who gathers all of the information, closes the door, scratches his chin, and decides that this is a stock that he wants in his portfolio. The process of picking stocks does not require anybody else's active cooperation.

Trading Costs

By our calculations at the Plexus Group, and we analyze data from 100 different investment managers worldwide, the one-way cost on a large-cap trade is about 1 percent—1.01 percent exactly. The commission fee is typically 6 cents a share (12 bps), market impact is about 9 cents a share (20 bps), delay costs are 24 cents a share (53 bps), and missed trades are 8 cents a share (16 bps). Missed trades occur when not all the shares that a portfolio manager orders are ultimately bought.

The average one-way cost on a small-cap trade (for a company worth less than $1 billion in market capitalization) measures out at 4.5 percent. These numbers are large enough to account for the difference between the results that active managers have shown on average and average index fund performance.

The commission and impact costs are the tip of the iceberg; they are readily visible to all, but they only represent 32 bps in total. About three-quarters of the total cost is invisible to anyone who is simply looking at the transaction tape. The hidden parts of the iceberg are the costs of delay and of missed trades. A trader looking to beat the volume-weighted average price or trying to minimize the impact will fail to see all the hidden costs (delay and missed trades) coming in. Yet these hidden costs are real costs. They leak out of invested assets. A portfolio manager who wants to sell a security that is moving down rapidly because bad news is out will incur real dollar losses in the portfolio as a result of delay and missed trades. With a buy decision, what the manager might have won in the way of performance is a little more ephemeral, but for a sell, real dollars leak out of the portfolio.

Few of the firms we have worked with have any idea about these hidden costs. The portfolio managers at these firms simply believe that if they pick the right stocks, they will win the performance game; the rest is plumbing. They cannot see that simple procedural changes can help performance. Without systematic measurement and reflection, they cannot identify trader skill and they cannot differentiate among brokers because all brokers say they provide best execution. What these firms do not realize is that differences between brokers can be measured—along with differences in the quality and the difficulty of the execution. Armed with this information, firms can justify paying a higher commission for one broker over another. A firm can say to a plan sponsor that is trying to direct 100 percent of the commissions to a no-name broker: "Dear plan sponsor, we can prove that this is in the best interest of your pension plan. There are other important things that the commission is designed to pay for, such as execution."

Commission Recapture

Commissions are used for many purposes, and they should be accounted for. The benefits of disclosure about commissions surely far outweigh the efforts. The average plan sponsor, however, does not see commissions in the same way. The plan sponsor's logic is often as follows: If the manager can use commissions from my account to buy services that she thinks are of value to me, why not use those commissions myself to buy services that I know are of value to me?

One municipal fund that I am familiar with has zero budgeted for purchase of outside services, such as performance evaluation. The fund has money budgeted for pencils, pens, and salaries, but it does not even have any money to pay the actuary. All outside services are supposed to be funded out of the commission. Is that an overload on the commission? It can be. The descent down the slippery slope starts when an unsuspecting plan sponsor believes that a manager who does soft-dollar trades can use brokers who rebate part of the commission back to the plan sponsor. If a manager can do a little of that, why not do 100 percent recapture? The whole *raison d'être* for the commission is lost.

In general, portfolio managers believe that directed trades hurt performance. They see obstacles to the smooth functioning of the trading practice. Unfortunately, all too often they cannot prove it to the satisfaction of their clients. The client is often suspicious that the manager is trying to hide something that benefits the manager but not the client, such as 12b-1 fees. Most plan sponsors believe that direction or recapture of commissions does not hurt the pension plan. They typically believe that best execution is defined the way it is defined on the floor of the stock exchange: that no better offer exists at this very moment. Obviously, in such a case, everybody gets best execution. And if all brokers provide best execution, then which broker a plan sponsor chooses does not matter, so why not try to recapture some of those "excess commissions?"

Plan sponsors fail to consider what happens when the trade exceeds available liquidity and a higher level of broker skill is required. How should best execution be defined for those situations? Again, the answer is $X - Y$, and doing this calculation for every trade shows that brokers do differ from each other in terms of providing best execution.

Order Flow for Nondirected Trades. Exhibit 1 illustrates the functional flow of trades when the client does not direct the trade—no recapture of commissions. The process starts with a portfolio manager's idea. Not all ideas are difficult to execute; some are easy. An easy trade often goes to a services broker or a third-party broker, who may hand it to a correspondent or take it directly to the floor of the exchange. The defining characteristic of this trade is that the broker waits for liquidity. The broker queues the order on the floor, and when the other side arrives, the trade gets done. If the other side of the trade happened to be there when the broker put it on the floor, all to the better. If it was not, the broker waits for liquidity, meting out the order to the market at a digestible pace—one that does not upset the balance of supply and demand.

The hard trades (anything that is more than half a day's volume) cannot be done the same way as easy trades; the broker has to go out and find the liquidity. The broker would probably look to the exchange to find parts and pieces of it on the floor. The broker would also look to his contacts to find a natural other side. Some brokers specialize in putting the buyer and seller together so that they meet and are able to execute. Some brokers will put up their own money and buy it from the manager to complete at least part of the order. The function of a good trade desk, of course, is to evaluate which of these processes makes the most sense in the search for liquidity so that the broker can complete this trade.

Order Flow for Directed Trades. Exhibit 2 shows what happens for directed trades. The trader may go to a broker who may be part of a much larger brokerage firm or who may simply specialize in soft-dollar commissions. Frankly, when we have evaluated the execution for directed easy trades, we have not found a lot of difference between directed and nondirected trades. In fact, they are quite similar in their execution ability. So, nothing is lost in the quality of the brokerage as long as the recapture is being done for easy trades.

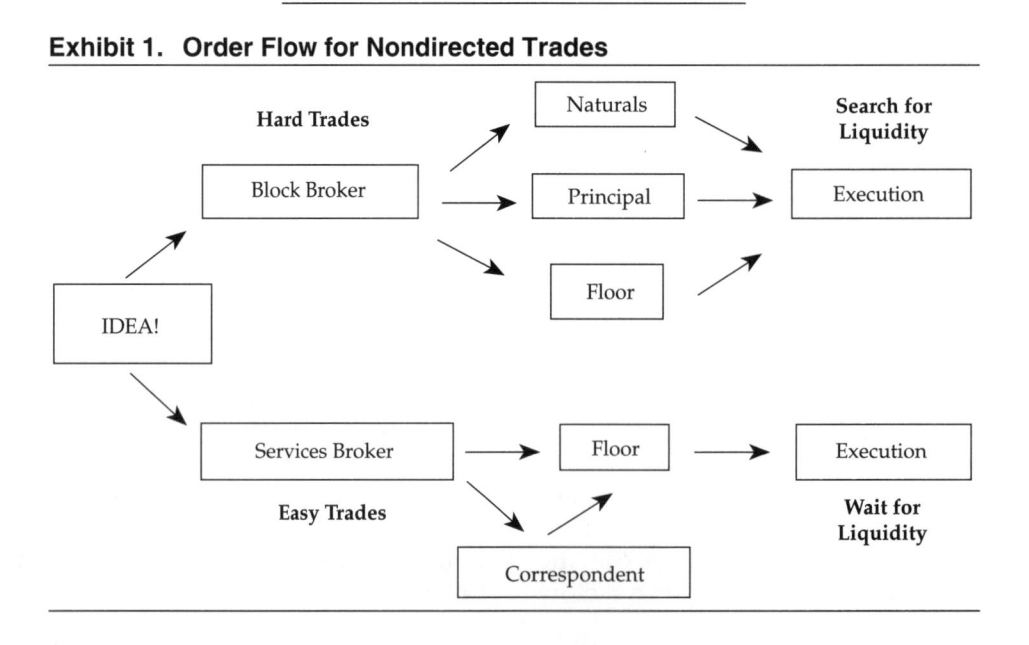

Keep in mind, however, that a manager does not manage just one account. A manager manages accounts for lots of different individuals, lots of different institutions. The law is silent about how to treat potential conflicts among clients. The law says a manager must act as a fiduciary for an individual pension

Exhibit 1. Order Flow for Nondirected Trades

Exhibit 2. Order Flow for Directed Trades

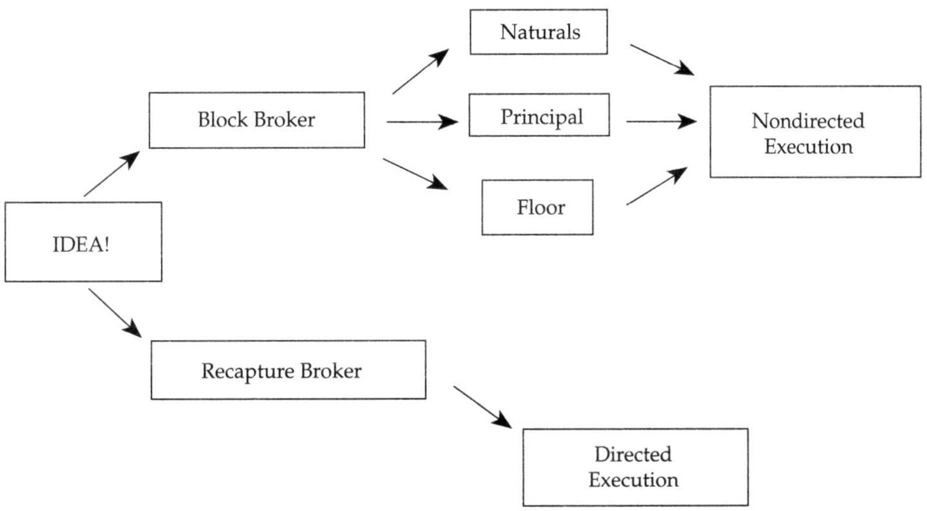

```
                      ┌─→ Naturals ──┐
                      │              ↓
        ┌→ Block Broker ─→ Principal ─→ Nondirected
        │             │                  Execution
        │             └─→ Floor ───────↗
IDEA! ──┤
        │
        └→ Recapture Broker ──→ Directed
                                Execution
```

plan, mutual fund, or client, but it does not say what a manager is supposed to do if he has, say, 100 clients to whom he owes a duty of best execution. In the spirit of the greatest good for the greatest number, most managers try to generate superior performance for every account. As a result, all accounts that trade on the same day typically get the same average trade price. A manager who has some clients that direct their trades is in a tough position. The recapture broker may be an entirely different broker from the one the manager wants to use to execute the block trade. So, who comes first? Somebody is potentially advantaged, and somebody is potentially disadvantaged. That is, somebody got a better price than somebody else did. Arguments have been made that managers ought to rotate accounts, which recognizes that a difference exists. But most managers if pressed will tell clients that trades with constraints on them will be sequenced last if it matters.

Suppose a manager has 1 account that is directing and 99 accounts that are not directing. The manager wants to trade 1 million shares into these 100 portfolios, of which 10,000 of the 1 million shares are going into the one portfolio that is directing. The manager does not want to telegraph to the marketplace (to those guys sitting staring at screens looking for exploitable trading patterns) that she is a continuing buyer in this stock. The trader will typically trade the block first for the 99 portfolios and then do the best job possible with the remainder of that execution through the directed broker. That approach makes sense from a fiduciary standpoint because the manager is always trying to do the best for each client. Note, however, that the directing account will receive a different, and often less advantageous, price. If Account A wants the manager to direct the commissions, doing so may affect Account A, but the manager cannot allow Account A's direction to disadvantage Account B. Account B should be kept whole and not affected by Account A's actions.

That was a simple example with only one plan sponsor directing to a particular broker, but most trade desks today have requests for dozens of different allocations going to different brokers in different places at different times. The result ends up looking like **Exhibit 3**. First, the block trade (the nondirected part) is done through naturals, principals, floor trade—wherever liquidity can be found. Second, the directed trades are done by individual directed brokers.

Problems with Directed Trades. Clearly, directed trades are a big impediment to effective execution because the whole trade could have been done as a block trade and then allocated to all clients at the same price.

A further complication with directed trades is that the trader might be directed to use an unfamiliar broker. The trader loses the ability to select the broker he thinks is most fit to execute this particular trade. The "best" broker is the one who knows the stock, knows where the sellers are, can principal a trade if need be, views the relationship with the money manager as important, and can be counted on in difficult trading situations. Such brokers can be described as having proven capacity, fidelity, and commitment. A major money management firm will trade with the major brokerage firms on an everyday, multiple-contact basis. The trust and belief that information is protected is exceedingly important to money managers. The continuing relationship is a reward to the broker for a job of continuing good work. In contrast, how could a

Exhibit 3. Order Flow for Multiple Directed Trades

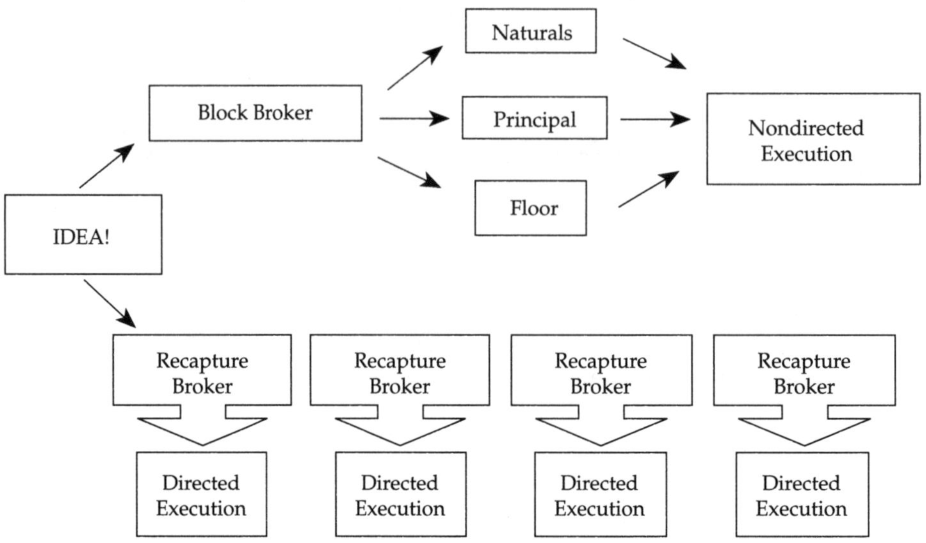

money manager reward a recapture broker whose fidelity and allegiance is to the plan sponsor and not to the money manager himself?

We have performed several studies on the effect of using directed trades. We look at the orders, trace through the part that was directed, and compare the trading performance with the part that was not directed. We have repeated this study about three or four times and always come to the same approximate conclusion: Every penny recaptured in a recapture process costs 3–5 cents a share in performance, as shown in **Table 1**. The place where it leaks out primarily is in delay and missed trades.[1]

Summary. Trades that require simple execution skills are fine for recapture or directed commissions. These are reasonable-size trades in large-cap stocks that are listed on an exchange and that are made in quiet market conditions. The structure of the market is designed to give equal execution quality to trades of that nature. Small, routine trades all get handled in the same manner. Most trades of less than 10,000 shares will be executed mechanically, and differential broker skills will be hard to detect. When direction is limited to those easy trades, plan sponsors can buy third-party services, such as performance evaluation, without incurring a performance penalty.

A hard trade, however, typically should not be done through a soft-dollar broker. Hard trades (large size, small-cap stocks, price momentum conditions) make up 10–50 percent of a manager's trading. Such trades need top skill brokers in order to be executed well. For example, if a manager's trade idea is based on a broker's recommendation, that manager is probably not the only person who the brokerage firm called with that recommendation. A lot of competition exists for liquidity. When competition exists for liquidity, the winner is not the one who gets the best price; the winner is the one who gets to execute first, if at all (i.e., liquidity considerations can dominate price considerations). How does that situation fit into best execution? Well, it fits into best execution by asking whether it provided maximum benefit to the portfolio. That is, did the portfolio benefit even though the manager paid a high commission?

Therefore, recapture can be justifiably done on easy trades, but it should not interfere with execution of the hard trades.

---

[1] Go to www.PlexusGroup.com for further information on this study, "Revisiting Directed Brokerage: Still No Free Lunch."

Table 1. Soft Dollars and Directed Brokerage

Trading Performance	Nondirected Trades	Directed Trades	Benefit of Directed Trades
Commissions recaptured	0.0¢	3.0¢	3.0¢
Easier trading	56.2	40.0	16.2
Cost over benchmark cost	4.5	16.2	–11.7
Delay and missed trades	10.3	–4.5	–14.8

Trading Issues

Trading today is becoming increasingly complicated, and the traders are in the middle. In trying to execute the manager's request, traders have to deal with a host of new issues and "interested" parties—compliance officers, clients, brokers, regulators, and evaluators. The result, in many cases, is conflicting interests, commission overload, and confused objectives. What is a poor trader to do? What is the objective of the commission? What activities should it be funding?

The answers can be seen by asking the fundamental question, whose decision is the trader trying to execute? The answer, obviously, is the manager's. The objective of trading is to improve performance. A manager thinks, "I like a stock that is not in my portfolio better than one that I have in my portfolio. I want to swap the one I have in my portfolio for the one that I do not have because I believe it will enhance plan assets and improve performance." The trader's job, then, is to actualize the manager's ideas. If the trades do not get executed, performance will suffer. If they are not executed well, the same result occurs—performance suffers.

Issues such as directed commissions and commission recapture are real but are secondary to the primary purpose of getting the manager's ideas implemented. They are distracting to the overall trading process. What can be done with commissions has to be controlled. It is the responsibility of the money manager to see that the use of the commission does not interfere with the primary purpose. Otherwise, assets will be splashing out of their containers.

Finally, if managers believe that transaction costs are trivial and unimportant, managers will be urged to trade a lot because trading (in these managers' opinions) does not cost much. Such managers will be urged to trade on thin margins, and their paradigm of thinking about the investment process and how they add value will be warped. In such an environment, performance suffers, and suffering performance is not in the best interests of clients.

Conclusion

Commission recapture can be a potentially serious impediment to best execution when it becomes insensitive to trading needs and creates queuing problems. Real dollar losses from using commission recapture can far more than offset the value of the commissions recaptured. Recapture may be neutral to performance, but it cannot systematically enhance performance.

Recapture also creates problems when the manager needs to respond to regulators. Under the Investment Company Act of 1940, the SEC conducts inspections to ensure that the advisor is in compliance with the securities laws and that the business activities are otherwise consistent with the information described in the Form ADV, which describes how the manager manages money. The inspector is interested in seeing if the actual behavior is in line with the expectations. SEC inspectors usually look at four things:

- What are the compliance procedures? Are they written down? How are they enforced?
- What are the brokerage and soft-dollar practices? Can the manager prove that they actually represent best execution?
- What is the procedure relating to account allocations? Is this procedure fair to all of the accounts?
- How do the wrap-fee programs work?

Interestingly, wrap-fee programs have the same problems as directed commissions in terms of the quality of execution. If a manager has to direct all of his trades through the broker who gave him the account to be managed, that broker does not have to earn the manager's business on a trade-by-trade, day-by-day basis. Consequently, performance can suffer.

Following are questions that managers should be able to answer about their trading programs:

- What is the total implementation cost? Where does it go? What does it buy for the plan?
- Are these costs reasonable? How do you adjust for the fact that sometimes you pay higher costs? How often does this occur? How do you control that process?
- How do you coordinate trading style with investment style? What trade-offs do you consider when choosing trading methods?
- How do you communicate your sensitivities about the speed and price of execution to brokers? Does it change their behavior? How do you monitor that change? Can you prove it?
- How much do you allocate to research? Is it a reasonable amount or is it excessive? How do you know when the allocations are out of balance?
- How do you assure that brokers are providing quality service? What do you do when you sense a problem?
- How do you validate your traders' skills? What are you doing to improve implementation skills?

The important point is that what is in the client's best interest may not be what an uninformed client might identify as in the client's best interest. That is, contrary to what many plan sponsors think, excessive recapture is often not in their best interest. What is in the client's best interest is to invest in a way that generates performance and that keeps costs under control, which means constantly monitoring to determine the best practice for executing trades.

Question and Answer Session

Wayne H. Wagner

Question: Should initial public offering (IPO) profits be included when measuring transaction costs?

Wagner: We include IPO profits when assessing the total costs. Getting hot IPOs is a considerable benefit of using a particular broker. If you are an important client of that broker, which means accounting for about $5 million a year in commissions, you will reap the benefits from that relationship. The benefits come in the availability of liquidity when there is a tight liquidity situation (and what is tighter than a hot IPO?), research, and so on. We have found that intensifying and closely monitoring a relationship with a broker improves the execution compared with scattering that execution across hundreds of brokers.

Question: What do you think about the long-term viability of the day-trading phenomenon?

Wagner: I think day trading is a frothy top-of-the market kind of activity except that the costs really have gone down.

Day traders can trade in a way that they could not have done, say, five years ago because of reduced costs and increased information availability. Ten years ago, the average clearing cost of a trade was roughly $20. That number is now about $2 and will soon approach zero, especially with T + 1 clearing.

Day traders can now execute rapid turnover tactics on a thinner and thinner information edge. They are getting execution within 5–10 seconds on all the trades they want to do, so they are able to execute on small bits of informational advantage. The gains in cost and informational advantage result from advancing technology, and they won't go away. My guess is that some of the day traders will do quite well for a period of time, but there are also sheep to be shorn among the population of day traders.

Question: How will the aggressive price competition in the retail trading environment spread to the institutional business?

Wagner: Electronic markets are beginning to have a big impact on institutional investors; 94 percent of the trading in Amazon.com are trades of less than 1,000 shares. An investment manager who wants to buy has to play in that ballpark. Traditionally, that kind of trading was done through consolidator brokers, who act as intermediaries between the retail market and the institutional market. But the retail market and the institutional market march to the beat of different drummers. Features that are valuable to a retail market, such as transparency, are a total anathema to an institutional market, which does not want the day traders to find out that they're trying to accumulate a big position in a particular stock.

Question: Have you looked at doing complicated trading strategies, such as long–short strategies?

Wagner: It is more than doubly difficult to do a long–short spread trade than it is to do one side or the other of a trade, because you have to coordinate the trade and because the restrictions on short sales sometimes prevent you from doing what you want to do. It is seldom a good time to be simultaneously buying and selling. From a trading standpoint, the long–short strategies don't seem to benefit from a lowered cost structure.

Question: What makes a trader a good trader?

Wagner: Experience. We were asked to evaluate the traders on a trading desk—about 12 different traders. We knew when the managers gave them the orders; we knew when they sent the orders to the broker; we knew all of the pieces that go into completing a trade; and we benchmarked the trades using our average-cost equation for each trader on this trade desk. That study clearly showed that the best traders were the most experienced traders.

Traders live in a rapid-fire, point-blank world. They must react instinctively, and that instinct comes only with experience and a natural talent to prosper in that fast-paced world. I admire them. Experienced traders seem to develop a sixth sense about what a trade smells like, what it feels like, and what seems like a good idea and what does not.

Question: What is a manager's duty when the client is compromising best execution?

Wagner: If you find that somebody, whether an individual or an organization, is acting out of ignorance in a way that is detrimental to his or her own interests, it is your job to educate that individual. The fact that that client doesn't know what the costs are represents, in my mind, an obligation to teach the client what is in the client's best interests.

Attracting, Motivating, and Retaining Professionals

Thomas J. Dillman, CFA
Senior Vice President, Director of Research
State Street Research & Management Company[1]

> A firm's investment culture is crucial to attracting key people and keeping them committed to the organization. A firm creates its investment culture through all the myriad interactions it has with its employees—recruiting, training, motivating, and measuring and compensating performance. A firm's culture, however, has to be monitored to make sure that it continues to support the ultimate goal—making sure the clients are happy and getting what they want.

The key to attracting, motivating, and retaining employees lies with a firm's investment culture. Culture is dynamic. It changes because relationships change, and relationships are forced to change because of external factors (such as a competitive environment) and internal factors. Any time a firm adds a new person to a group, for example, the composition and the dynamics of the group change. Sometimes a person has the opportunity to set up a firm and mold its culture, but most people work in firms that have established cultures and history.

In this presentation, I will go through several topics on investment culture—defining, creating, and managing the investment culture. Under each of these topics, I will cover a variety of issues that pertain to the day-to-day functions involved in trying to create an environment that people want to come to, work in, and give a large portion of their life, effort, time, and professional dedication to.

Defining the Investment Culture

A firm's culture has a lot to do with attracting key people and keeping them committed to the organization. A firm's goals and objectives set the tone and establish the framework in which all other components of building a culture are defined. Other factors defining a firm's culture include its clients, its products, its organization, and its investment process.

Goals and Objectives. Corporate goals and objectives vary widely among firms. Some firms strive to maximize their clients' wealth or to grow the assets or profits of the firm. Others try to maximize the owners' or partners' wealth or the job satisfaction of the professionals working in the firm.

Clients. The nature of the clientele—who the firm has chosen to have as clients—has a lot to do with defining the culture and the nature of the organization. The culture of a firm varies considerably depending on whether its clients are individual investors (such as trust beneficiaries, wealthy individuals, or mutual fund investors) or institutional investors. A trust bank, for example, has a particular clientele that creates a certain tone and type of service. Dealing with institutional clients has a different tone, in which consultants define, in many ways, the relationship between the money manager and the plan sponsor.

Products. To a certain extent, products are based on both the kind of clients and the goals and objectives a firm has. In the 1950s and 1960s, managing pension fund assets was the big growth area. Since the late 1970s, mutual funds have been the great growth vehicle. Mutual fund growth appears to be slowing down; only the top five firms seem to be gathering any money lately. Now, firms want to manage a clientele of wealthy individuals in a cost-effective way. The kind of clients a firm has naturally leads to the type of products it offers—whether a single product line or multiproduct line, institutional versus individual, growth versus value, small cap versus large cap, and so forth.

---

[1] Mr. Dillman is now Director of U.S. Research at Scudder Kemper Investments

Organization. The way a firm is organized defines how the firm and culture function overall. The key issue is structure. Does the firm have independent portfolio managers who compete with each other? Or does it have a group of portfolio managers who work collectively either in a team or a loose sharing arrangement? What is the role of research? Do portfolio managers do the research, or are specific analysts assigned to specific industry groups? Does the firm have a central research department?

The structure of the firm defines the job functions for portfolio managers and analysts and the relationships among people, and the relationships determine the culture of an investment organization. How people relate with each other on a day-by-day basis in the pursuit of professional and personal objectives determines which firms people choose to work at and stay with.

Investment Process. The culture is ultimately defined by the investment process, which brings together all the components involved in how decisions are made and what steps are followed in collecting information, building a portfolio, and generating returns on behalf of clients. The goals and objectives of the firm, how the firm defines and services clients, what kind of products the firm uses, the structure of the firm, and how relationships are established—all funnel through the investment process.

Creating the Investment Culture

A firm creates its investment culture through all the myriad interactions it has with its employees. Thus, recruiting, training, motivating, measuring performance, and compensating performance are all important aspects of creating the investment culture.

Recruiting. Recruiting, or attracting the right person, involves matching the person's skills and personal goals with the needs of the firm. Not all M.B.A. candidates want to work at State Street Research. I have met many bright and talented people who should work at Fidelity Investments, whose culture is different from ours at State Street Research, and I have met other people who would hate to be at Fidelity and would probably like our firm because it is collegial and sedately entrepreneurial, not aggressively entrepreneurial. In looking at a firm, people consider whether the culture is attractive and able to satisfy their professional goals.

Recruiting is becoming a bit of a problem because more and more talented young people are being drawn into the technology field rather than finance. For the first time ever in my 20 years in management, I have heard that people are not showing up for job interviews. Many people seem to believe that starting a company is easier than joining an established investment firm, getting a CFA charter, and working their way up the ladder. Such beliefs are presenting considerable challenges in the recruiting area. At State Street Research, we use different recruiting strategies for entry-level analysts and experienced analysts.

- *Entry-level analysts.* For entry-level positions, we hire one or two people with M.B.A. degrees each year. These people are given immediate coverage and responsibility in order to accelerate their learning curve and our return on our investment in them. We also have a program for bringing in research associates. Associates are often people with B.A. degrees who first got jobs in accounting or mutual fund sales so they could eventually go into research or portfolio management. They do a lot of the spreadsheet work and conference calls and can thus gain experience by supporting analysts and portfolio managers. Being a research associate is a great learning experience, and because our recruiting program includes internal interviewing and hiring, having such a program gives us the opportunity to train our people and potentially move them into analyst positions.

- *Experienced analysts.* Recruiting for experienced analysts requires a different strategy. We use a combination of professional recruiters and business contacts. Recruiting experienced talent is not always easy; at times, we may have to accept trade-offs to get the person we want.

For instance, we are currently looking for someone to run our technology team—somebody with a broad understanding of technology who can manage the group. The technology area, obviously, is very important. We have a number of talented people, but in my judgment, they do not have enough experience to manage the team. In this case, we have retained a professional search firm, a recruiter who is combing the entire country in search of a technology analyst with the specified criteria.

Hiring a technology analyst is not only a very, very expensive proposition today, but it also potentially involves trade-offs in terms of other aspects of our firm's culture. One problem is location, which is typical of certain industries; a lot of technology analysts want to be in California, where everything is happening. One of our criteria in building a culture is to create a team, which becomes difficult if the team members are physically united only occasionally and if most communication occurs via e-mail and telephone. To say that team building can be done only with face-to-face interaction may be an anachronism. Some companies do everything electronically, and their people are dispersed all over. Nevertheless, we do not want to hire a person to be a technology analyst who is going to stay in California and manage people in Boston. We may get to the point where we have to accept that limitation to get the right person, but I do not think it would work.

Using existing business contacts is an alternative to using recruiters (and paying their relatively exorbitant fees). In most places, the rumor mill is fantastic. In Boston, everybody knows everybody and is aware of what is going on: Who is leaving what company, who is dissatisfied, and so on. As soon as people heard that we were looking for a technology analyst, we had 20 calls from local people. Sometimes we can find the kind of person we want through local contacts. In fact, we have just hired two people—an energy analyst and a banking analyst—who we learned about through our contacts.

Another alternative is to hire people from industry. Sanford C. Bernstein & Company, for example, hires top-notch people from industry to provide information to the portfolio managers, who then translate the analysts' expertise into good stock selection, but that is a different model and a different culture from ours. Because we want analysts who can pick stocks, we want people who can translate their expertise immediately into a valuation on a stock; we do not want to wait for someone to get up to speed; we do not want to take a chance that the person might not be a good investor, even though he or she may be an expert in the field. So, hiring from industry is not an option for us.

Training. Building a culture, not just a firm, means building teamwork and relationships. New people, whether they have experience or not, need to be shown the way things are done, so an introduction to a firm's culture should be part of the training process. Our training program involves mentoring, immediate responsibility, and the CFA Program.

■ *Mentoring program.* Recent M.B.A. graduates and new research associates need to be taught some of the skills that they may not have acquired. Emulation, which is basically the model for all learning, is one of the best training techniques. A mentoring program, however, is more than having new people observe and mimic those around them. Assigning professional people to work with new people, whether they are experienced or not, is a powerful acculturation tool.

Part of our mentoring process for new hires involves what I call the "three points of contact." First, I assign the person to a senior analyst who has some expertise in the area in which the person will be working. The senior analyst shows the new recruit how to analyze companies and make judgments on stock valuation. I also assign the person to a senior portfolio manager, because I want the inexperienced analyst to understand the perspective of a portfolio manager, who has to decide whether a stock fits in a portfolio. The third point of contact is me. I make sure the other mentoring relationships are working and do quality control to make sure things are on track, and when they are not, I get involved and come up with ways to get them back on track.

■ *Immediate responsibility.* After I assign mentors, I quickly give the new person some responsibility. I can have a new analyst covering an industry within three months; this person will be the one who makes the recommendations on the stocks. At State Street Research, we have a culture in which the portfolio manager is the one who makes the decisions for the portfolio. So, an analyst who has been with us for only three months has to deal with a culture in which his or her recommendations may not be accepted as quickly as those of a more experienced analyst. Notwithstanding that bias, the new analyst has to get up in front of the portfolio managers, make the presentation, field the questions, go back and do the extra work, and then, like all of us, live with the consequences of his or her recommendations. Analysts are either right or wrong, and everybody knows it; part of the learning process is feeling the pressure of this business. This trial-by-fire method is the best way of putting new analysts into the culture in which they will perform in the future. If they are going to contribute to the firm, I want them up and running as quickly as possible.

Sometimes a person is not quite ready for this responsibility. My job is to make sure we have hired people who are smart and have good work experience, but we never really know if they can do the job until they do it. For example, I once had a young man who had been with us for 18 months. I had difficulty managing the issue of his performance; he was not doing well, but I could not tell him specifically what he could do to improve. He simply did not get it. He could not pick a stock to save his soul, and I did not know how to help him. He did the analysis but drew the wrong conclusion time after time. I told him that if he did not get it in six months, I would recommend that he go on to something else. This was a case in which the person was not tracking, and I ran out of ways to help him. I spent a year working with him making sure he was paying attention to the details; talking to him about valuation, timing, and psychology; and giving examples of how it is done by pointing to other people in the firm. Fortunately, once I told him his job was in jeopardy, he quickly improved. So, I learned something too; perhaps I had been too lenient and supportive.

■ *CFA Program.* The CFA Program is one of the best solidifiers of knowledge and experience a financial professional can have in the investment business. After getting a master's degree in education and graduating from business school, my boss at that time told me I had to get my CFA charter—something I was not familiar with. I did not want to do it, but I did. After going through the program, I realized that it took everything I had learned or heard about in school, and everything I was learning at work, and put it into a broad, meaningful context. Most people I have talked to agree that it is quite a good program in terms of tying together their understanding and knowledge, stimulating their thinking, and giving them a broad context in which to evaluate what they are learning on the job.

The program is a requirement for all research associates and M.B.A. degree holders at State Street Research. Interestingly enough, most of the M.B.A. candidates I have interviewed have already taken Levels I and II of the CFA exam, and in some cases, they have already completed the program. These people recognize that the CFA Program is important to many employers.

Motivating People. Everything in this presentation has to do with motivating people. A culture that is good for clients, that generates good investment returns, and that compensates people competitively is a culture that will motivate people.

This industry attracts smart, motivated people. Such people will be attracted to a firm that offers them an opportunity to actualize their personal and professional goals, which vary from individual to individual. So, the culture has to support the individual's professional goals as well as the individual's personal lifestyle goals. Offering competitive compensation, obviously, has to be part of the package. These days, being competitive is getting very expensive—especially when hiring a good technology analyst. To get a good technology analyst, a major money management firm has to pay something approaching seven figures, and half of that for somebody with less experience. A firm has to be competitive, and it has to make decisions on the basis of what it needs and what it can afford. Money management firms are always in a scarce-resource-allocation situation, but somewhere in the array of expenditures, a portion of money has to go toward remaining competitive, which means offering a compensation package that attracts the kind of people the firm wants and needs.

Measuring Performance. How to measure performance is at the heart of any performance-oriented business, whether it is professional sports or investment management. I firmly believe that job descriptions must be "operationalized." In other words, I have to tell people what I want them to do before I can expect them to do it, which sounds obvious, but I have observed on numerous occasions, in business as well as personal situations, that people sometimes presume that others simply know what is expected of them.

By operationalizing the job description, I can define the job in such a way that I can measure performance and specify the payoffs for success. Being explicit, as opposed to vague, puts the manager in a better position to help people improve their performance and make a greater contribution to the firm and clients. Relying on some amorphous definition of what doing well means and presuming that people will voluntarily generate reports or that analysts will have conversations with portfolio managers or that portfolio managers will share information with other portfolio managers probably will not get the desired result.

Define the job, and then measure performance according to the way the job has been defined. The definition should be measurable or documentable, and I like to publicize the results of the measurements.

With a performance-oriented culture, we can still be collegial and team-oriented and offer a nice place to work, but the bottom line is performance. We have to deliver to clients. One way to get people thinking in terms of performance is for them to know that their performance is being measured and made available to everybody. We calculate the 1-day, 5-day, 30-day, quarter-to-date, and year-to-date performance of every fund and publish the data in our *Daily Notes*. Each fund manager's performance is included. We look at the absolute performance as well as the benchmarks so that we can figure out how a manager is doing relative to the benchmark. Similarly, we calculate the analysts' performance, and these results are made available to the analysts and the portfolio managers. Everybody knows how everybody else is performing. And everybody knows they are in a competitive environment.

My role is to use the performance data remedially, not punitively. If something is not tracking, I can go to the analyst and ask what happened: "You picked one bad stock, and it completely killed you. What did you do?" As an example, I had an analyst who had a tendency to always "swing for the fences" and go out on the risk spectrum. Out of 10 stocks, 5 would be winners and 5 would be just disastrous. More often than not, the relative performance was down. I worked with this analyst and told him that he could not always go for "home runs." To continue the baseball analogy, I told him that I wanted him to try to get singles, doubles, and triples, even though sometimes he would strike out or hit into an out. I told him if he was going to play the game, he had to do it across the spectrum. Therefore, I use the numbers to help analysts understand where they have gone wrong and where they can go right, and publicizing these numbers helps analysts gain that understanding.

Therefore, what gets measured depends on how the job is defined. How the different measures are weighted depends on how the firm wants to encourage its employees' behavior. How the firm wants to encourage its employees' behavior depends on what objectives it has. And all of those issues are interrelated and come together in the culture of the firm.

Compensating Performance. No one likes to be evaluated, but everyone knows that being evaluated is important in achieving professional and personal goals. Because people get nervous about evaluations, how a firm goes about doing evaluations is an important aspect of creating a culture in which people feel good about their environment. Equally important is creating a compensation structure that motivates employees and encourages them to stay.

Analysts. For our analysts, quantitative measures make up 60 percent of the potential bonus. These measures are as follows:
- *Buy/sell spread.* The spread between the buys and sells should be positive to add value to the portfolio managers in terms of an analyst's recommendations.
- *Hit ratio.* The hit ratio measures the percentage of recommendations that were correct versus all the recommendations that were made. A portion of the analyst's bonus is based on how many percentage points over 50 the analyst has achieved. In a research firm, if nobody can get over 50 percent, the firm might as well use a coin or a quantitative black box. Analysts are there to add value, to get house odds versus player odds. During the past several years, our department has achieved about a 55 percent hit ratio, which is a good result collectively.
- *Analyst fund performance.* The performance of the analyst fund—a real, live portfolio—is another quantitative criteria for assessing analyst performance. We evaluate the analyst's performance in managing his or her own portion of the fund and translate that information into a compensation measure.

Qualitative measures make up the remaining 40 percent of the bonus. Qualitative does not mean subjective. It simply means using something other than strict performance numbers to measure performance. In our case, we use observations. Are memos getting written? Are earnings estimates up to date? Are voicemails and e-mails maintaining a flow of information? Are analysts doing their jobs as analysts? Are they working with fellow analysts? Are they working with fellow portfolio managers?

We also use two broad qualitative measures for analysts: one measure coming from the portfolio managers and one from the research director. Portfolio managers always want new ideas, and they want analysts to keep them informed about what they are following in their portfolios. To encourage analysts to work with that goal in mind, portfolio managers are given an opportunity to evaluate each analyst in terms of their relationships with the analyst and the analyst's specific impact on their portfolios. Because the analyst does not have control over the end result (i.e., which stocks the portfolio manager includes in the portfolio), evaluating an analyst's performance in a strict quantitative fashion is difficult. Our approach to measuring performance in this area is interesting. Once a year, we ask each portfolio manager to rank each analyst on a scale of 0 to 100, with the percentage reflecting what that portfolio manager believes our firm should pay in terms of the percentage of the analyst's potential bonus. We also ask the portfolio managers to explain why they have given a particular ranking. We look for a good, solid performance of 75 percent. Somebody who scores 90–95 percent is doing very well, obviously better than somebody who is doing 70 percent or 65 percent. Every portfolio manager has a chance to talk about each analyst, and we do this review as a group, allowing the portfolio managers to revise their numbers or add a comment after hearing their colleagues. I take notes.

The second half of the qualitative score is the research director's evaluation, which has two key components: an assessment of the quality of research and an analysis of the analyst as a team player.

Portfolio managers. A similar quantitative and qualitative approach can be used to evaluate portfolio managers. I do not manage portfolio managers per se, but I have strong ideas about how to do it. The primary objective is for portfolio managers to outperform their benchmarks and peers and to provide good relative returns to clients. So, a lot of emphasis should be put on those measurable results. Depending on how the firm has defined itself and the kind of client base it has, the compensation approach can include or exclude the portfolio returns versus peer index or include both the peer index and the benchmark. The following quantitative measures can be used:
- portfolio returns versus benchmark index,
- portfolio returns versus peer index,
- compliance with risk guidelines, and
- new business success.

The first two criteria are fairly typical quantitative performance measures. The third criterion deals specifically with managing risk. In determining the compensation level, we have considered including an evaluation of whether a portfolio manager keeps the risk profile within a certain range, which we define as tracking error, but we have not yet implemented such a measure in the actual determination of compensation. Finally, if portfolio managers are asked to go out in the market and bring money in to grow the asset base (the fourth criterion), a portion of their bonus should reflect their contribution to the asset base from new inflows.

Qualitative measures for portfolio managers depend on how a firm wants to define its culture, what it wants to track, and what kind of investment process it is trying to generate. Two qualitative measures are information/idea sharing and investment leadership/mentoring. In particular, a firm might want to encourage portfolio managers to share any information they get from phone calls, conversations, or meetings with company management. A firm might also want portfolio managers to exercise investment leadership by actively telling others what they are buying and why. And finally, a firm may specifically want to measure, qualitatively, how a person does in setting an example for other people, both experienced and inexperienced.

■ *Compensation.* For a compensation scheme to be effective, it must include payoffs for success and consequences for failure.

In most firms, the payoff for success includes both quantitative payoffs (which tend to be financial) and qualitative payoffs (such as promotions, additional responsibility, and/or ownership). Most firms offer a base salary and a performance bonus. In some cases, firms give certain employees the opportunity to share in profits, either as owners or as quasi-owners (i.e., phantom owners). Some of the more creative approaches in this profit-participation area are in terms of options, phantom stock, and so forth.

In terms of promotions, the investment industry is a fairly flat business with few opportunities for promotion; not a lot of differentiation exists. Firms have analysts and portfolio managers. But within those narrow levels, promotions are sometimes important for distinguishing who has done well. People need benchmarks to know that they are doing well and moving along. In a flat organization, it is hard to find the kinds of labels, signals, and symbols that acknowledge the progress people are making, so we have a couple of different titles and are expanding them. A lot of people say titles do not matter, but it is interesting how many people bring up the desire to be promoted behind closed doors. They are looking for differentiation, a signal that they are doing well, and they want that signal to be conveyed to other people.

I consider management responsibility to be a form of compensation. Some people would argue that being asked to be a manager is almost a negative, but most people recognize that being asked to manage means that they have been given additional responsibility. They have been given charge of other people's futures, which differentiates them from the people who are being managed. Although a firm with two principals and a secretary might be successful (they may know how to manage money), they do not necessarily know how to manage a firm. Problems can arise when such people retain control over the management of the firm and do not hand it over to a professional manager who can organize the process of building a culture.

Ownership participation offers another chance to reward someone for success and includes the opportunity to buy into the firm or to get profit-sharing shares, phantom stock, or options.

Establishing consequences for failure is an important part of creating and managing a culture. One of the hardest things to do is to tell somebody he or she is failing or has failed. But doing so is important not only for the individual but also for the firm, the clients, and the state of mind of fellow professionals, because if somebody is failing and there are no consequences for failure, then the rewards for success are diminished. Acknowledging someone's failures becomes even more important when people start to evaluate that phenomenon in light of the competition in a highly aggressive world.

That being said, if someone is failing, I consider that person to be my responsibility. I either hired or "inherited" the person, and my job is to find a way to make that person's value to the firm greater than it is and to keep that value from falling. My first response is to find a remediation process for the person. We sit down and talk about what the problems are, and I make suggestions about specific issues. In some cases, I tell the person what he or she should do. In other cases, the solution is very broad, such as signing up for the CFA Program and learning more. I help people craft questions to ask managements or join them on a company interview. I help them develop a program for improving their performance or at least going through the process whereby they can improve. I cannot improve people. They have to improve themselves, but I can help them do that.

If performance does not improve, the manager has to communicate that it is not getting any better. In this litigious world that we live in, to get to the point of saying "I am sorry. You failed, and you no longer have your job," the manager has to have a documented record, especially for "special" cases, such as people older than 40, women, minorities, the handicapped, and so on. It is probably a good practice for a manager and for a firm to have a process by which people know that the manager has given them time, specific suggestions, and help. The manager should give warnings, let people know that they are in trouble, and give a deadline for improvement. The manager should have some intermediate steps before getting to termination. Demotion is an option, but I do not like to use it. The point can usually be made with a private compensation adjustment if necessary. If that does not work, then termination is the only option.

Termination is very difficult and very painful. It is easily the most difficult thing any manager has to do. The way I console myself is by knowing that I have exhausted every opportunity to help the person remedy the situation. My job is to make sure that everybody who is working for me is making a positive contribution to the firm and to the client. If I come to the conclusion that a person is not making a positive contribution, or is making a negative contribution, it is easier to go to the next step. If I have given this person every opportunity and have come to the conclusion that this is not the right place for that person, and may not be the right business for that person, I tell that person. I recommend seeing a career counselor and thinking seriously about whether this is the role the person is suited for. And sometimes, just a change of firm and a fresh start is all that is needed to rejuvenate a career.

The idea is that to get the most out of talented people, managers have to treat them well and care about them. Even if they need to be let go, treat them well, respect them, honor them, and be honest with them. A manager should say: "I am not firing you because I do not like you. I am terminating your job here because you have not made a contribution to the firm, and that is the job." I have had people thank me for firing them, because in the end, I helped them, and I helped the firm.

Managing the Investment Culture

A firm's investment culture does not exist by itself; it must be managed. Managing a business organization, managing the people, and then also managing the investment process is very difficult. Some people can manage the business and the investment process; personally, I find that difficult and have opted for managing the business and the people. Nonetheless, the person managing the business must be seen as someone who understands the business—managing money and making stock selections.

Probably the most important thing for a manager to do is to lead by example. How a manager behaves defines in many ways the culture that he or she is able to establish. Ethics is part of the culture at State Street Research. We believe that we have been a good, upstanding investment management corporate citizen; we pride ourselves on that fact, and we let people know it.

A crucial element of managing culture is dealing with the people. In a certain sense, investing is not a team sport. It comes down to how someone does against the market, but I believe that good managers and good firms can leverage the talent of individuals so that the sum of their contributions is greater than just adding them together. Managers and firms can accomplish such synergy by supporting the individual at every turn. I spend most of my time talking with people. Having an interest in what they are doing is germane to the firm. Managers should get to know the people they are supervising and focus on the individuals so that they are more willing and more content to work within the cultural environment that the firm has already defined and established.

Cultures change over time. Good firms' cultures have to be monitored to make sure that they continue to be relevant and supportive of the ultimate goal—making sure the client is happy and getting what he or she wants. Otherwise, the firm itself and the people who work there will be undermined. The firm will not be successful.

Conclusion

A successful investment culture is defined, created, and managed in the mutual interest of the clients and the owners of the firm. Obviously, different firms define investment culture differently. Some people have a very succinct definition of culture—what is good for the client.

We depend on clients, and they have come to us because they need us. The way we maintain their allegiance to us at State Street Research is by providing a culture that ultimately achieves its objective. How a firm makes decisions depends on a lot of different things, but ultimately, those different components lead to the building of a culture that supports the best interests of the firm, the professionals in it, and the client.

Question and Answer Session

Thomas J. Dillman, CFA

Question: How does your performance as research director get evaluated?

Dillman: My performance is based on a number of different components: firm profits, equity department investment returns, assessment of research department performance by portfolio managers, assessment of my performance by portfolio managers and the head of equities, and performance of the Analyst Fund, which I manage.

Question: Which firms do you regard as having strong research departments and why?

Dillman: Wellington Management Company, Capital Research and Management Company, and J.P. Morgan & Company—all of these have differentiated themselves on the basis of their long-term commitment to research, and two have dedicated research departments where analysts are encouraged to become experts in their industries. Their success as firms is a testament to this commitment to research.

Question: What considerations would you emphasize in determining whether a service can be paid in soft dollars?

Dillman: The key criterion is whether or not it provides "research" that can be used in the investment decision-making process. Economic analysis, market analysis, or models for valuing stocks would qualify; data on competitor performance, when used by portfolio managers in analysis of their portfolios, would qualify. But having the marketers use the same information might be questionable.

Question: Please give examples of how teamwork has added value to your research effort.

Dillman: For our Analyst Fund, two analysts who follow industries in the consumer area voluntarily made overweight/underweight decisions, which required one to cede investment dollars to the other. The bet, however, paid off for the overall portfolio.

Often, portfolio managers become privy to information that is germane to analysts or other portfolio managers; dissemination of such information is an example of teamwork.

Managing Firm Risk

Bluford H. Putnam
President
CDC Investment Management Corporation[1]

> Managing risk is a constant challenge, partly because managing risk does not mean eliminating risk but rather balancing risk and return opportunities in the best interests of clients or investors. At the most basic level, managing risk is about continuously updating risk forecasts to help in the management of both the investment firm and client portfolios. Moreover, one of the most fundamental concepts is knowing a portfolio's worth at all times so as to develop an intuitive sense of the dynamic activity in financial markets and to appreciate the changing patterns of risks in the portfolios managed by the investment firm.

Hardly a week or month goes by without some serious financial mishap in the asset management industry reminding everyone about the importance of managing the risks in the portfolios for which an investment firm is responsible. This presentation begins with an intuitive rationale for one of the most important, but sometimes forgotten, issues in risk management, namely, keeping an eagle eye on the worth of all of the portfolios in one's care. Then, I will try to provide some perspective on the differences between risk management in the banking industry and risk management in the money management industry, which I hope will clarify some of the critical subtleties in the application of risk management techniques in the real world, as opposed to discussing theoretical issues that may or may not be relevant for day-to-day risk management. This topic leads into a discussion of where the asset management industry is going in terms of risk reporting, and finally, I will offer some concluding thoughts on the importance of combining risk measurement systems and quantitative risk models with managerial judgment to further improve both risk-adjusted portfolio performance and client and investor relationships.

Enhancing Risk Intuition through Real-Time Portfolio Monitoring

Effective risk management of an investment firm and of the portfolios managed by the firm requires that all the people involved in the whole portfolio process develop an intuitive sense of a portfolio's performance numbers. It is important to realize that everyone can be helpful in risk management—not just the president of the firm or the chief investment officer (CIO) or the head of risk assessment or the portfolio manager or the marketing person or the back-office executive, but everyone. The key to involving all of a firm's employees in the risk management process is making real-time and daily net asset values on every portfolio widely available inside the investment firm.

The underlying business management agenda for making real-time and daily net asset valuations on every portfolio available and widely disseminating them in the firm is to build within the staff, from the top to the bottom and back to the top, an intuitive sense of the patterns of risk that develop in ever-changing financial markets. Building a culture of risk intuition is not easy, and identifying in advance whether someone will develop an intuitive sense for patterns of numbers is also difficult. A degree in mathematics guarantees nothing; someone can have an intuitive sense of theoretical mathematical concepts without having an intuitive sense of whether a number is right or wrong or whether a number fits into one pattern or another. Similarly, a strong accounting background does not seem to guarantee number intuition either. Only by regularly focusing on portfolio numbers can someone start to understand how the numbers move and to build an intuitive sense of the patterns of risk in the various portfolios and financial markets as a whole.

---

[1] Mr. Putnam is now president of Bayesian Edge Technology & Solutions, Ltd.

©2000, Association for Investment Management and Research

Thus, knowing a portfolio's worth at all times, minute-by-minute—or at least real time as much as possible—is important to risk management because it helps portfolio managers and everyone involved in the risk management process to develop an intuitive sense of what is happening in the portfolio relative to the dynamic nature of financial market activity. With fancy computers and telecommunication systems, investment managers can obtain useful real-time estimates of a portfolio's worth and volatility. They simply plug a client's portfolio into Reuters, Bloomberg, or some other system, and the technology can show the portfolio's value changing in front of their eyes. Looking at the real-time and daily price changes of a whole portfolio—watching what is going on during the day as well as the daily returns—gives a sense of how the portfolio will respond in particular market conditions and how much risk is in the portfolio. Paying attention to the effects of different market conditions for a long period of time gives money managers a unique experience that may turn out to be much more valuable to the investment firm and to its clients and investors than any quantitative measure of risk.

Knowing a portfolio's worth also gives risk managers an appreciation of what part of the portfolio's return is real—that is, could be realized—and what part is fake, or unattainable. For example, say I, as the chief investment officer, am passing through the trading room and I see a great profit number on the screen for one of the portfolios. Perhaps I want to grab that profit, but the trader says we cannot realize it because most of that reported P&L (profit and loss) is located in Japan and the Japanese market is closed. Before we can take the profit, he explains, certain Japanese economic data will be announced and the Japanese market will also react to the U.S. data already announced, and the resulting reaction in the Japanese market will most likely mean that the profit (the one I am seeing on the screen) will be gone by the time the market reopens. The point is that for many real-time P&Ls, a lot of the reported numbers cannot be realized at that specific instance in time. By looking at the P&L continuously on the screen, however, managers begin to get a sense for the profits that can be taken and the profits that are imaginary. The markets can move quickly, so more profits may be imaginary than people think, and this intuition of the true profit and risk picture is a valuable perspective to build into the culture of an investment firm, especially one that trades in illiquid securities or in global portfolios, which is almost everyone these days.

Daily P&Ls—not to mention online, real-time P&Ls—also reduce operational risk, which is an important reason for disseminating in the firm the real-time and daily net asset valuations on each and every portfolio. Doing so means that lots of eyes are watching the numbers. In fact, such real-time and daily portfolio valuation information is probably the single most important factor in reducing operational risk. When the daily number looks wrong, it usually is wrong, but the operational and valuation team can fix it within 24 hours if someone can see, for example, that a trade was not reconciled properly or was put into the system incorrectly. Thus, the errors do not build up over the month or get hidden in the normal volatility of the portfolio.

Even the mathematics of the formulas used to calculate the simplest of things can come under increased scrutiny in this process. For example, determining the one-month forward rate on a currency may seem to be a straightforward calculation, but the asset manager's or investor's internal software systems for valuation may calculate it differently from the system used by the custodian. That is, the two may use different mathematical algorithms for interpolating points on a yield curve, which can result in different estimated interest rate spreads for interpolated maturity points in the forward currency valuation process. If many people in the investment firm are looking at the numbers regularly, then when large forward currency positions are added to a portfolio, even small discrepancies among different valuation systems can be identified and the whole valuation and reconciliation process among different systems can be improved.

A story about the importance of paying attention to patterns of numbers on a regular basis comes from an episode at the U.S. Federal Reserve that occurred a long time ago. The Fed stipulates that anybody who works at a bank must take two consecutive weeks of vacation a year. The theory is that if someone is committing fraud and is out of the bank for two weeks, somebody else will find the fraud. About 20 years ago, in the late 1970s, one of the clerks in the Federal Reserve Bank of New York was taking the required contiguous two-week vacation at a time when the money supply data were very important for the market. The substitute clerk received an erroneous number from a large bank for that week's deposits. The number was off by an extra zero, turning hundreds of millions into billions. Simply running one's finger down the column of numbers from previous deposit reports from this bank would have shown the mistake, because the new number would have literally stuck out from the column. But the replacement clerk did not do that, and the numbers entered the compilation system incorrectly. This oversight led to a multibillion dollar mistake in the weekly money supply data, which, in turn, blew the data off the charts. It also blew the bond market off the charts the day it was announced. It eventually blew executives (not clerks) out of jobs. Although this is not an example from a money management firm, it does underscore the point that having the entire staff of an investment firm develop a sense of the portfolio data is an important part of building a risk management culture that runs from operational issues all the way through to portfolio design and execution.

In summary, the entire staff of an investment firm should be considered part of the risk management team, not just the CIO, the head of risk management, or the portfolio manager. If all the people involved in the portfolio process are paying attention to the portfolio numbers on a regular basis, then they naturally will develop an intuitive sense of what is going on, which, in turn, will help them alert the appropriate risk managers to unusual behavior, which is critical to managing risks and minimizing errors.

Bank versus Fund Risk Management: Not the Same Game

Knowing the worth of a portfolio all the time is a surprisingly unappreciated part of managing risk. But equally important is understanding the risk management biases that have crept into the risk management process in the banking industry and that may actually increase the risks for investment firms if they apply banking risk management approaches blindly (or more likely, hire bank risk managers to become fund risk managers and get stuck with the inappropriate biases by accident). For fund managers, risks must always be estimated and assessed in a portfolio context and balanced against the return potential of the portfolio. Banks take a different path for risk management, and asset managers need to be aware of the difference. Bank risk managers focus mostly on the possibility of disaster in individual transactions. They also focus on quantitative risk measures taken from daily data to build risk projections of how much money can be lost in a single day.

This emphasis in bank risk management on individual transactions and on a very short-term time horizon for risk estimation means that relative to an investment firm, not enough attention is paid to the longer-term risk characteristics of the whole portfolio, involving both the correlation structure and the upside profit potential within the whole risk–return distribution.

Please note that these bank biases are not necessarily inappropriate for the specific task at hand, but similarly, bank risk management processes are not always appropriate for the risk management processes of an investment firm. Following are some examples, as well as a discussion, of why the differences do (and should) exist between bank and fund risk management processes.

Probability of Risk of Loss: To Be Biased or Not? Bank risk managers spend a lot of time looking at the probability of disaster for each transaction and spend considerably less time analyzing the risks to a portfolio of transactions. There is a good reason for this practice. A bank, or the capital markets group of a broker/dealer, makes money by earning commissions or fees on each and every transaction. Once a capital market transaction has occurred, if it requires some form of continued involvement or management by the bank or broker/dealer, the objective is to hedge the risks and protect the commission or fee that has already been earned. That is, once the transaction has occurred, the profit has been made, and the bank just wants to keep it. The bank is not expecting to earn further profit from the management of a hedged position. Thus, bank risk management teams have the job of trying to measure the risk of a big loss in any specific transaction. They want to know whether one event, and what type of event or position, could sink the whole ship. Banks are appropriately, but myopically, focused on this major issue.

Furthermore, bank risk managers have an incentive to be very conservative. The people who work in bank risk management departments typically do not receive bonuses for making money for the bank. In addition, compensating a risk manager for the absence of losses from positions that were not taken is virtually impossible, because they cannot be measured. But, of course, these people can be punished for losses on risks that are accepted by the bank. This asymmetric incentive system means that risk managers always want to eliminate or reduce potentially large losses by not letting the position be executed or the trade be taken in the first place. They do so by putting a high risk assessment on each position. The result is that the risk managers keep their jobs, the bank avoids large losses, and, oh yes, the bank forgoes many profitable transactions and the sales and trading teams enter into a culture of us-versus-them, in terms of the risk management team.

What has happened is that bank risk managers have adopted a policy of being intentionally conservative in assessing the risk of a big loss. All of the incentives are designed to provide reasons for overestimating risks or estimating risks to be larger than they may actually be in reality. As a result, in a bank, the risk managers avoid, like the plague, making an educated and unbiased guess about an unknown risk; and if forced to guess, they purposely exaggerate the risk, introducing a conservative bias to their risk forecasts. Money managers, however, are always making educated guesses about the risk–return trade-offs in every position and every portfolio, and it is in their best interests for these risk forecasts to be unbiased.

The following hypothetical example from the world of behavioral finance helps to illustrate the difference. Suppose I tell a banker and a money manager that I have an urn containing 50 red marbles and 50 blue marbles. I tell them that if I draw a red marble, I will pay them $1,000; if I pull out a blue one, I will pay them nothing. I then ask them what they would pay me to play this game. They calculate that they should not pay more than $500, or 50 percent of $1,000. Because the probability distribution of returns is known, both the banker and the money manager are comfortable calculating the risk because they have a complete understanding of the probability distribution.

Now suppose I change the game. I tell them that if I pull out a red marble, they have to pay me $1 million; if I draw a blue one, I will pay them $500,000. The returns are intentionally skewed, and now a chance exists for a big loss. Furthermore, this time, I have added a random number of red and blue marbles to the urn, so the true proportion of red marbles to blue marbles is unknown to everyone. Now, I ask them how much they would pay to play, or in this case, how much I should pay them to play this game. Pulling out a red marble would break the bank (lose $1 million). The players do not know the probability distribution of the red and blue marbles, so they must guess the shape of the probability distribution of returns. This is a very uncomfortable position for the bank risk manager and common practice for the money manager.

Our money manager, who is well versed in Bayesian statistics, knows that if the distribution is unknown, then a guess, given the information at hand, of a 50/50 distribution is a good starting point. The money manager will expect to be paid $250,000 or more to play the new game (50% × $500,000 – 50% × $1,000,000). Our banker might be equally well versed in Bayesian statistics, but the banker doubles or triples the risk assessment of a loss because of the incentives the bank has placed on the risk manager. So, the banker assigns an 80 percent probability of pulling out a red marble (the outcome that will sink the ship) as an intentional overestimation or conservative estimation of the risk of loss.

By the way, the banker's assessment of the risk of loss also implies assigning a 20 percent probability to pulling out a blue marble. In practice, however, the bank risk manager probably would not bother to assign a probability to a blue marble being selected, because doing so would not be in the job description. If the banker did assign a probability, he might base his estimate on the (unbiased) nature of the game and assign a 50 percent chance to a blue marble, which would violate the laws of probability for the total probability distribution because the probability of pulling a blue marble plus the probability of pulling a red marble out of the urn must equal 1.

At any rate, because the banker is focused on the risk of downside loss only and intentionally overestimates the risk of loss, instead of making an educated and unbiased guess, the banker is implicitly underestimating the potential for a gain. And, in this case, the banker will want $700,000, at least, to play the game (20% × $500,000 – 80% × $1,000,000).

In this example, the banker would demand a higher payment from the game master to play than the money manager would. In the long run, over many games, the money manager would do two things: First, the money manager would constantly update and continuously revise her estimation of the probability distribution (in case the 50/50 initial guess was wrong), and second, the money manager would keep playing the game. A very high probability exists that the money manager will generate a fair and reasonable return from the risks being taken by playing the game over and over again. On the other hand, the banker will not win the bid and will not be playing the game. The banker will also not be earning a reasonable return on the risks that could have been taken by virtue of wanting, at a high cost in terms of long-term return on equity, to avoid a large loss on any one transaction.

The point is that although bank risk managers can simply double an unbiased guess about an unknown risk to avoid a large loss on a single transaction, money managers cannot simply double the risk and accept the conservative bias in their risk estimation. They must focus on continually playing the game in such a way as to produce the best risk–return ratio or to get the most return from the risks they are taking. In addition, money managers clearly care about the probabilities of winning big, not just the probabilities of losing big. They like setting up positions with fat tails to the right of the distribution and (occasionally) making a lot of money. Such portfolios are not impossible to have, but they do require that the money manager know about the whole probability distribution.

A related point is that some risk managers do not like to use standard deviation as a measure of risk because it penalizes them for upside volatility, for which they cannot gain as a risk manager. But a money manager should carefully assess that upside (gain) volatility, in the sense of having an investment process that actually tries to create it. Hence, the duty of the risk assessment process in an investment management firm is to look at both profit and loss potential and to estimate the whole distribution, not just the fat tail to the left (loss).

Money managers are trying to maximize their information ratio—that is, maximize the return of the portfolio over its benchmark divided by the risks taken. In this context, it should be obvious that to maximize the information ratio, money managers have to think about the whole probability distribution. It may not be normally shaped; it may have some fat tails or some asymmetry. But whatever the shape, money managers must think about the whole distribution—not only about a large loss. Moreover, money managers cannot be biased. If money managers are consistently conservative—that is, if the probabilities assigned to risk are always too high—those managers will consistently not invest enough. Money managers who consistently do not invest enough will not make enough in return, will have ratios of return to risk below everybody else's, and although they may not necessarily be fired, they will not be good managers. They will be mediocre (or worse). And they will lose clients, or their marketing teams will not raise as much money as they would like. The key is understanding that clients are not providing money so much as they are providing risk-taking capability, and overly conservative managers are depriving clients of return for that capability. Money managers need to get the excess return above whatever benchmark has been set in relationship to the risks they are allowed to take.

If somebody asks me to put $100 million in a money market fund, clearly, that person does not want to take much risk. If she asks me to put $100 million in a long/short global hedge fund, she obviously has an appetite for risk. As a portfolio manager, I need to measure the activity in the client's portfolio in terms of the client's risk-bearing capability and provide a return that is relevant for the amount of risk I am allowed to take. If I am too conservative, I will not take enough risk, and I will not generate the return that will show up over time as a satisfactory information ratio or Sharpe ratio.

Transaction versus Portfolio Analysis. Bankers tend to look at every transaction as the point of analysis rather than the whole portfolio. They do so for a reason. Suppose someone in the bank's capital markets group sells someone a swap. The bank takes a fee or commission and books a profit on the transaction. The bank does not want to lose this profit, so the people on the risk analysis and hedging team develop a hedging strategy for the position that remains on the bank's books as the other half of the swap that has been sold to the client. They are managing the risk so they will not lose any money, but they are not trying to make any more money. From the bank's perspective, it took its fee or commission at the front end of the transaction and has already booked its profit. For the bank, the remaining exposure on its books is a necessary evil from the nature of complex capital markets transactions, but it is a zero net present value position—managed in a way to preserve the profit already made, not to make further gains.

Following is another example that illustrates the risk–return nature of how a bank does its business. If a company goes to a bank for a loan, the company knows it will get either a fixed interest rate or a floating rate over some benchmark with the spread fixed. The bank wants to make sure it is paid the agreed fixed rate of interest or the agreed spread. What the bank now wants to avoid is the loan going bad. If the company goes bankrupt, then the bank owns the company, and bankers do not want to own companies. The bank is not trying to make any more money on this deal, but it is focused on making the expected profit if the interest and principal of the loan are paid on time and in full. For the bank, the profit decision has been made (in the decision regarding how much interest or spread to charge) and the objective is not to lose it. The risk management team is charged with assessing the risk of loss to help set the credit premium and then with monitoring that risk over time. For the bank, the loan has become a short put option, on which it has received the option premium, and now it is hoping it will never have the underlying assets put to it, as would happen if the borrower were to go bankrupt and turn over its assets to the bank instead of repaying the loan. From this illustration, one can easily see why bank risk managers are so focused on estimating (and usually overestimating) the risk of a large loss.

In contrast, asset managers invest in portfolios to earn future returns; they are not trying to earn commissions or fees on individual transactions. Money managers will certainly not make the right decision on every security in their portfolio; there will always be some winning and some losing positions. Individual wins and losses matter less, however, than how the whole portfolio does. What also matters is how much risk is in the whole portfolio. If managers take positions that offset risk in some way, they get credit for minimizing risk in the total portfolio. Furthermore, positions are not paired in a risk-reducing sense. That is, a bank wants every transaction hedged so that it can keep the whole fee or commission as its profit. The fund manager is, however, interested in whether a new trade increases or decreases the risk (and return) of the whole portfolio, regardless of whether the new trade is paired with an old trade or not. In thinking about portfolios, every incremental position has a degree of risk reducing or risk increasing potential relative to the whole portfolio and thus must be assessed in the context of the return potential of the whole portfolio. And as money mangers are well aware, the portfolio is expected to be composed of positions that on average, and over time, are net positive present value transactions. The profit is in the future.

To consider a whole portfolio, managers have to think about how various positions are correlated, so they get different answers about risk from the ones bankers get. Correlations are not stable and are hard to predict, but if money managers do not think about correlations, they will not get their risk–return analysis right. Correlations are important because they allow managers to diversify. Professor Harry Markowitz got his Nobel Prize in economics for pointing out that if a portfolio has a lot of *different* risks, the portfolio will benefit in terms of reduced risk for the same expected return. The less correlated the risks are, the less total risk the portfolio has and the better the overall portfolio will be in terms of its return potential for each unit of risk taken. By and large, risk managers in banks rarely think about correlations because they are focused on individual securities. Whereas bank risk managers treat each transaction as a zero net present value exposure, money managers are always expecting a positive net present value. Money managers thus balance risk and return as part of the investment process. Banks, however, have separated the return function and risk function by taking the return from each transaction as part of the front-end fee or commission (which, by the way, the money manager is paying to the bank). In short, risk management is a different game for banks and investment firms.

The Daily Data Trap. Bankers tend to focus on daily data for their quantitative assessment of risk. As discussed at the beginning of this presentation, watching real-time and daily net asset valuations of portfolios is critical to gaining an intuitive sense of the risks being taken. But as the primary input into a purely quantitative risk assessment process, daily data can be dangerous to one's financial health.

Daily data are a banker's favorite input into risk information tools. The BIS (Bank for International Settlements) wants to know how much a bank can lose in a day, so its guidelines favor banks using the past 100 days of daily data in at least one version of the value at risk (VAR) calculation. Broker/dealers also ask this question in the sense of VAR. For example, does a 1 percent chance exist of losing $100 million today? Bankers and broker/dealers want to know how much money is at risk today—for one day.

In the fund management world, daily data are not necessarily beneficial as the primary inputs into a purely quantitative risk assessment process. Using high-frequency data (such as daily data) as inputs into a risk assessment system can alert a manager to changes in risk and other things happening in the market, but they can also be dangerous if they are depended upon as the primary measures of risk.

For example, suppose you are running a global portfolio and you are underweight French equities and overweight U.S. equities (or in the hedge fund context, you are short French equities and long U.S. equities by the same amount). Suppose that in the morning all of the equity markets are showing gains around the world. You will be making money in France and losing money in the United States. If the correlation is high between these two markets, nothing is happening in your portfolio; the gains in one market are offsetting losses in the other. Or the overweight position in one market might be providing positive excess returns above the benchmark while the underweight position is providing negative excess returns, thus offsetting any relative gains against the benchmark.

Now, suppose that after the French market closes at midday U.S. time, the U.S. Federal Reserve Board (Fed) raises rates unexpectedly (or by more than the market anticipated) and the U.S. equity market dives. You will lose money in the United States but nothing will happen to your French positions because the French market is closed. According to the prevailing practice of most banks, money managers, and custodians, when a market is closed, yesterday's price is used. In this case, however, one would use today's closing price for France (the price prior to midday U.S. time) and the closing price for the U.S. market (the price at the end of business U.S. time). The next day, your P&L reverses because the market in France opens and follows the previous afternoon's action in the United States. If you look at the P&L during the evening of the first day, your daily data will show a large loss and considerable volatility, but you know that neither the loss nor the volatility is real because the rest of the world is going to react to the Fed move the next day.

For global portfolios, historical daily data, such as that used to calculate the previous 100-day VAR, almost always increase the measured risk assessment of the total portfolio relative to its true risk. Such use of daily data in global portfolios means underestimating correlations by driving a wedge between the two markets that is not real because the daily data are for different closing times. Using daily data for risk management is less of a problem if the portfolio trades only in the same time zone, if it never uses leverage, and if it never takes short positions. Once different time zones, short sales, or derivative securities are involved, daily data will show more risk in a portfolio than it really has, which means that the investment firm will not take enough risk and will not earn sufficient returns to satisfy its investors.

Another problem with using daily data is that holidays around the world vary—and some countries have far more holidays than others. Holidays cause stale data, and stale data cause problems in VAR calculations based on historical data. Various approaches have been suggested to overcome this lack of reality in daily risk numbers. One common approach is simply to average two days, which is a crude but workable system. Using weekly or monthly data would be better, but the main point is to get away from using daily data as a primary risk assessment measure for portfolios that are longer-term in nature.

Risk Reporting

The asset management industry is moving rapidly toward providing more information about its risk-taking activities to investors and clients than it has in the past. In the future, Internet-based systems for reporting to clients will increase. This trend was driven by the demands of institutional clients initially, and eventually, it will also be fully available to retail clients or investors. In fact, investors or clients are probably going to get more risk information than they want, although they can always sort through it and take only what is useful for them.

In the first stage of enhanced risk reporting, most of the risk information will be derived from the historical performance of portfolios. This type of historical risk information can be termed "performance-based risk data." By using the time series of historical returns, risk-reporting software will easily be able to report on a variety of commonly asked questions about portfolio performance. Consequently, investors will be able to acquire an intuitive feel for the historical riskiness of a given fund or portfolio. The risk-reporting software will be able to take, say, the monthly returns of a portfolio or a fund and allow the investor to ask questions about the worst month, the best month, the VAR of the excess returns based on historical data, the VAR of the excess returns relative to a specified benchmark, the information ratio based on historical data, and the correlation of the excess returns with the benchmark. Institutional clients very soon, and retail investors eventually, will be able to have these questions answered in a flexible, drill-down, interactive Internet-based performance and risk-reporting system.

The second stage of risk reporting involves an analysis of the current portfolio or, say, the end-of-the-month portfolio. In this more-forward-looking approach to reporting risks to investors, the money manager will be revealing, to varying degrees, the risk factors or risk characteristics contained in current (or recent) portfolios. This risk reporting is unlikely to involve a complete disclosure of exact positions, but it may well give investors a considerable amount of information about the type of risks being taken, the relative diversification of the portfolio, the performance of the portfolio under certain specified stress conditions, and so on. This type of risk-characteristic reporting, which goes well beyond performance-based risk reporting, will be the standard of the future within a few years. Institutional, and yes even retail, investors are going to demand a greater understanding of the types of risks they are taking, and they are going to demand methods for monitoring those risks through time—after they make their investments.

The company doing the best job of developing risk-reporting systems for use by asset management companies is NetRisk—a software and risk management consulting firm located in Connecticut and New York. After taking data from the asset manager's returns and some data about portfolio risk characteristics that the asset manager provides, NetRisk puts the information on the Internet. The money manager's clients dial in, put in some passwords, and then they can see what the asset management firm is doing in terms of the types and levels of risk-taking activities. Although they cannot see the actual positions, they can see the risk exposures and a lot of information about the firm's performance history. By using NetRisk's Crystal Box® product to provide both performance-based risk reports and risk-characteristic reports, an asset manager's actions become more transparent to the investing community, which is good for clients and good for the industry. It raises the bar of transparency, openness, and disclosure while still allowing the money manager to have the confidentiality necessary to effectively manage complex portfolios in dynamic markets. Systems such as Crystal Box are the wave of the future.

Risk Judgments

The most important thing a risk manager does is make judgments, or forecasts, about future risks. Risk managers hate the word "forecasting." Many risk managers think they are in the business of measuring risk only from a historical perspective, which means that they analyze historical data and report on what the risk was. They are wrong if they think that is their job. A fund manager does need to know what the risk was, but the fund has already been bitten by that risk. So, more importantly, the fund manager must have an understanding and a view about what the risk will be. The investment firm requires a risk team that can help portfolio managers actually *manage* the risk in the portfolio. Money management is about making a risk (and return) forecast. The risk management team has to use judgment to be of any real assistance, because risk measures based on historical data alone are incomplete and often misleading. The concept of forecasting risk is new to a lot of risk teams because they do not distinguish "management" from "measurement."

Risk teams may be called risk "management" teams, but in reality, they have no portfolio management duties. In fact, these teams should be called risk "assessment" or risk "measurement" teams, because they are providing tools and judgments for use by the portfolio managers in running the portfolio and for use by the CIO in making sure that the portfolio managers are doing their jobs without taking too much (or not enough) risk.

One illustration about why judgment is necessary comes from the common tendency of volatility to be mean reverting. That is, the market goes through a storm, and then comes the calm after the storm. If that period of calm is long, managers should be scared. Bad things are probably about to happen. February, March, and April of 1994, for example, were the worst months in the bond market since World War II. What preceded them was 18 months of the fed funds rate fixed at 3 percent. The standard deviation (based on monthly data) of something that does not move for 18 months will mislead managers into thinking they have no risk. Based on historical data, bond managers had the least amount of risk just before they experienced the riskiest period the modern bond market has ever had.

Another example began in late 1997. The Asian Contagion started in October, and by December, people were starting to ask how risky the markets really were. Perhaps they were about half as risky as many risk managers were proclaiming because those infected markets—particularly the emerging markets—were trading at half price. Some of them were trading at less than half price. So, a lot of the risk was out of the market. Although the historical risk data went up, the events of October 1997 greatly lowered the risk in the next period.

The same situation happened in 1998 with Long-Term Capital Management (LTCM) and the hedge fund world. When LCTM blew up, credit spreads around the world widened. They were not all historically high spreads, but they were big spreads. A lot of scared people pulled back from the market, but that was the wrong response. This period offered a great opportunity to make a ton of money because much of the liquidity risk of otherwise high-credit-quality securities had been taken out of the market.

Money managers who use only historically based VAR measures will always be in the wrong place at the wrong time. They will be taking too much risk when they should be taking less, and they will not be taking enough risk when they should be taking more. A weather forecaster has to look out the window to see if it is really raining. Money managers have to look forward. Is an election coming up that could destabilize the markets? Is a court decision coming up that might change the market? Sometimes, the date on which a decision will be made is announced, so managers know when a volatility-inducing event will occur. The actual decision may not be known, but managers know a decision will be made and a stock will move—one way or the other.

Firms need forward-looking forecasters of risk to supplement all the historical data available. Managers need judgment to know when to stress test the forecasts. Most risk measures in the industry depend on normal distributions, but the normal distribution does not capture fat-tailed distributions, so the measures are flawed. The way to deal with this problem is to stress test the projections.

Indeed, judgment is playing a larger and larger role in risk management. People in the industry are dropping, appropriately, the idea that only one measure of risk exists—there never was and never will be. They are also questioning the idea that the whole risk process can be automated. A lot of it can be automated, but somebody with judgment is needed to interpret the findings and pull out the things that are important.

Risk managers are also starting to understand that commonly used models of risk measurement, such as 100-day historical VAR measures, can *introduce* tremendous risk into the system because, to various degrees, they encourage simultaneous risk-reducing behavior. That is, if everyone tries to reduce risks at the same time, then the liquidity risks in the system may be increased; the door for risk-reducing trades may simply be too narrow to accommodate the rush as everyone's 100-day historical VAR system sends the same warning.

Conclusion

Managing risk is as much a combination of art and science as managing a portfolio is. Those responsible for the risk management of a portfolio (whether portfolio managers or a risk management group) must have a sense of a portfolio's numbers on a daily basis, not only to make sure that a portfolio is on track (e.g., a trade has not been missed and performance is within normal ranges) but also to gain an intuitive understanding of the patterns of risk-taking activity under different market conditions. Also, an overreliance on daily data as inputs into risk measures should be avoided because daily data often show deceptively high volatility, resulting in the money manager not taking enough risk to earn the expected returns.

Risk managers must be forward looking. Using historical data certainly tells the manager about the risk that has been in the portfolio, but the manager also needs dynamic and forward-looking estimates of the risk that can be encountered in the future.

Numbers and quantitative analysis are certainly important in risk management, but so are qualitative judgments and forecasts. If the risk team is to be of any long-run usefulness, it must provide information that helps the CIO manage the portfolio managers and the portfolio managers design and implement portfolios that earn reasonable returns for the risks being taken. Finally, keep in mind that managing risk does not mean eliminating risk. Only by accepting a certain level of risk can investors achieve a certain level of return; managing risk means managing that balancing act. It takes judgment and skill, not just historical data and fast computers.

Ethical Issues for Today's Firm

Question and Answer Session
Bluford H. Putnam

Question: How would you explain the widening risk aversion in the U.S. markets—as in the risk premium for the stock market vis-à-vis the risk premium in the junk-bond market?

Putnam: In the financial markets in the latter half of 1999, we saw some increase in risk aversion in both equities and credit spread products, even if the people in Washington, DC, think there is less risk aversion. The regulatory community, particularly the Fed, appears to have taken the view that the stock market is too high, that investors are not paying enough attention to risk, and that people are investing blindly.

I do not think that is true. The spreads in the junk-bond market are still fairly wide. They have narrowed since the disaster of 1998, but as of the end of 1999, they still provided quite a bit of protection for the risks being taken. In equities, the second half of 1999 was unusual in that only a few companies or sectors led the whole market. Some parts of the stock market never caught up. So, some interesting risk premiums have appeared in sectors that have been left behind. This development is a positive one for a market; in some sense, it is evidence that the market is paying attention to risk in a reasonable way.

Going back to the credit sector, part of the reason for the risk premiums is liquidity. Broker/dealers are providing less capital than they used to provide for proprietary trading and to warehouse positions for eventual sale. In 1998, when LTCM went down, I thought LTCM was the problem and that after three or four months, the credit markets would return to some sense of normality. The credit markets did start to come back, but not nearly at the speed I thought they would. Even one year after the LTCM crisis, some credit spreads did not come back to normal levels.

My new theory is that LTCM was not so much the problem as the first casualty of the reduction of liquidity by the broker community. When the Goldman Sachs Group went public, it announced it would be putting less money into proprietary trading. When the Travelers Group bought Citicorp and Salomon Brothers, the first thing Travelers did was shut down the proprietary trading group in New York City (i.e., Salomon), which, by the way, had many positions similar in nature to those owned by LTCM.

Many banks and broker/dealer firms have pulled back from providing liquidity to the market. The result is a reduction in the market's buffer, so bid–ask spreads have to be wider and daily prices will probably be somewhat more volatile. Risk premiums for short-term investors will probably rise, and returns for people who have a true long-term horizon will rise. That is, someone who can be a provider of liquidity to this market can earn returns that are abnormal compared with recent history (not abnormal in the economic sense). Those liquidity providers are getting fully compensated for taking those risks, but the risk is the measured mark-to-market risk for short-term holding periods, not the risk of losing money for long-term investors.

Question: When marking to market in illiquid portfolios of securities, should one subtract a discount from the last traded price?

Putnam: This question relates to stale pricing in illiquid markets. What you need is a fair and reasonable price. As I understand the guidelines for mutual funds, the board of directors of the fund approves a policy that prices the portfolio in a fair and reasonable way. In the U.S. equity markets, usually the fair and reasonable price is the closing price. But for an emerging market position, a mortgage-backed security, or even an equity that doesn't trade often, such as a small-cap stock, if the last trade wasn't anywhere near the end of the day (in the case of a junk bond, the trade could have been last week), the custodians tend to take the last price on their computer system. A lot of things might have happened since the security traded at that price, however, so you should adjust the price but not necessarily take an automatic discount.

In addition, I would not take an automatic discount because doing so definitely hurts the current investors in relation to the new investors coming into the fund. The fund has an obligation to come up with the fairest price, not just to mark the price down because the manager is scared. To mark down a price, you must believe that the fundamental value isn't there or that you can't realize the value over a reasonable horizon. Illiquidity is not a good enough reason to automatically discount a security.

The automatic discounting approach to valuing illiquid securities can also be seen as another example of bank versus fund management thinking. The bank is internally marking its own portfolio. If the prices are marked too low, only the bank itself pays the price.

©2000, Association for Investment Management and Research

The fund manager is marking portfolios that belong to the firm's clients and also defines the entry price for new clients. The fund manager has an obligation not to favor old clients over new clients in marking the portfolio. Marking a security too low is a clear advantage for new investors, just as marking a security too high is a clear advantage for old investors who are smart enough to liquidate at the high prices.

Question: With the repeal of the Glass–Steagall Act, will bankers have to start thinking more like asset managers?

Putnam: Yes, they will. Banks are running portfolios, and they will wake up more and more to that fact. Actually, asset managers may simply buy banks. Insurance companies will buy banks because managing assets is what insurance companies do. Such acquisitions are already happening.

A bank's portfolio is very messy. A traditional bank that concentrates on making loans (not many such banks are left) has a portfolio of short put options: The bank makes a loan to a company; the company has the right, but not the obligation, to give the company's assets to the bank instead of paying the interest, which it would do, of course, only if the company wasn't doing well. The downside for the bank is that it gets stuck with the company. The bank has no upside. An upside would be if the company was doing really well, it would go to the banker and say, "I know we agreed to pay you 8 percent on that loan, but we're going to give you an extra 10 percent." The situation exemplifies the hockey stick diagram—a fixed interest rate plus a downside—which in the textbooks is termed "short a put option." So, banks better start behaving like asset managers, and they better understand the correlations in their portfolios rather than continue to focus on one disastrous scenario.

Question: How do various risk measurement systems calculate the risk of using leverage?

Putnam: Some hedge funds use a lot of leverage in their portfolios, so they are often asked to calculate leverage. Unfortunately, there is not a good answer or method. The problem is that a money manager may buy, for example, a futures contract that is long a certain market, such as the S&P 500 Index, and the manager may sell a futures contract that is short a highly correlated equity market. If one adds up the gross leverage, it may look like 4:1 or 5:1, but that position does not entail much risk. A relative-value risk exists between the two equity markets, but that is nothing like the risk in the equity market as a whole. So, one may look at some net measure of leverage (e.g., shorts minus long positions in an asset class), but this may be very misleading about the risk that can be contained in certain relative-value positions. All in all, I do not worry too much about leverage, but I worry a lot about measures of total risk and stress test results.

Competitive Challenges in the Investment Management Industry

Charles B. Burkhart, Jr.
President and Founder
Investment Counseling, Inc.

> No simple equations exist for calculating a firm's productivity or its success, so pinpointing the factors that make a firm competitive is a critical, but often ignored, issue. Another equally critical issue is for firms to realize that as the investment management industry evolves in this Internet-based world, so do competitive measures. For example, those firms that do not adopt a technology infrastructure and those that do not keep up with industry standards for compliance and for measuring investment performance risk being left behind in the offline world.

The competitive challenges facing firms is one of the most underserved topics in the investment management industry. It is rarely written about. It is rarely analyzed. It has nothing to do with acquisitions, high-end compensation, or Glass–Steagall, but the day of reckoning is coming.

In this presentation, I will discuss the competitive challenges facing an investment management firm—from the traditional measures of success to the impact of the Internet.

Competitive Measures

At Investment Counseling, the issue we care most about is what makes firms competitive. Our annual operating study "Competitive Challenges" provides an overview of organizational compensation, profit-and-loss statements, distribution, client service, and other measures of running a firm.[1] The study includes 80–100 firms that run the gamut from small, private-client lifestyle and boutique firms to large, multiproduct global enterprises.

The lead questions in the study are what makes a firm competitive and what makes a firm successful. Not surprisingly, the three most frequent answers are asset growth, revenue growth, and profitability, with more than 60 percent of firms selecting each of these factors. The answer that surprises people is firm size. Reports from the major brokerage and investment banking firms talk about the benefits of being a large firm and how firms compete on the basis of size and scale. After studying the issue for 10 years, however, I have found that size is one of the least important determinants of success in the industry. Only 36 percent of the firms in our study thought size had a high impact on their ability to measure success.

Productivity is curiously low on the scale of factors that have a high impact on a firm's ability to be successful, with only 22 percent of the firms selecting this factor. The reason might be because the investment management industry is one of the toughest industries in the world for people to measure its productivity. Measuring productivity for the airline industry is easy: When the plane takes off, how many seats are taken? Measuring productivity for lawyers is also easy: How many hours did the lawyer bill this week or this year? But what is the wasting asset in asset management? Is it capacity? Is it revenue or expense per employee? People are attuned to productivity measures today, and in the next 20 years, I suspect that productivity will shoot up and become a high-impact measure.

Beyond measuring success, we spend a lot of time considering how people think success is determined. The top factor is client service, with 84.2 percent of the firms selecting this factor; investment performance is second at 82.5 percent. Employee satisfaction (at 25 percent) rated strikingly low. How can so many firms think that employee satisfaction has so little impact on determining their success? Whether

---

[1] To download a copy of our 1999 "Strategy Challenge," go to www.competitivechallenges.com/html/home.cfm.

for a 5- or 500-person firm, employee satisfaction will rocket up in the next 10 years, primarily because of start-up firms. During the past five years, we have increasingly seen people who are unhappy with where they work start their own firms. These are not just small-firm incidents; even people at the biggest firms are leaving to start their own firms.

Interestingly, almost half of the firms surveyed thought that pricing had little impact on determining success. Does that finding mean that pricing is elastic? Only by segment or channel can elasticity of pricing be measured. Elasticity does exist in the high-net-worth business—the $10 million, $15 million, and up segment. But in the low-margin, commodity-like, low-tracking-error institutional business, very little elasticity exists.

When we talk about what the world will look like 10 or 20 years from now, we say that client service will still be important but that product capability will diminish somewhat because, inevitably, returns will revert to more normal levels. Although we will not go back to the old world of relatively static growth, caused largely by investment performance with some net appreciation resulting from additions and minimal withdrawals, investment performance will not carry the day or be the salve for all wounds.

During the past five years, an increasing proportion of managers' growth has been coming from the market and less from net new assets, as shown in **Figure 1**. In 1994, virtually all of the growth was coming from net new flows (as evidenced by the wide gap between the gray and white bar). But by 1998, only about 20 percent of the growth was coming from net new flows (as evidenced by the narrow gap between the gray and white bar). Consequently, if a

Figure 1. Asset Growth from Net New Flows and Market Appreciation

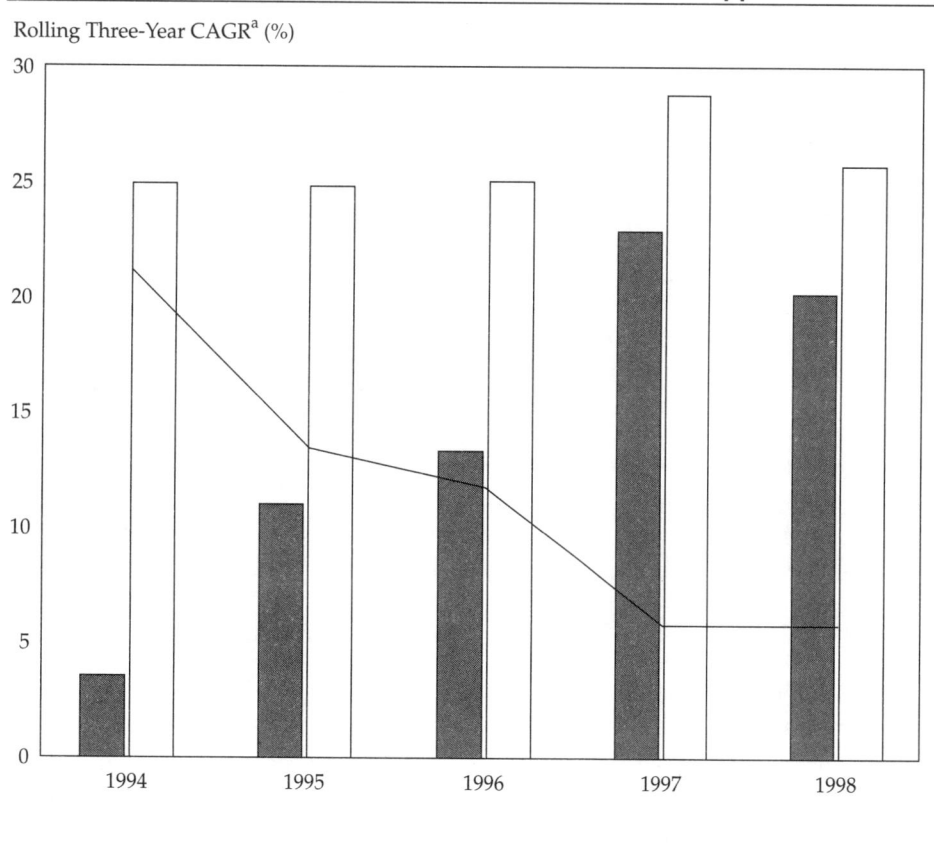

Rolling Three-Year CAGR[a] (%)

■ Weighted Three-Year CAGR: 70 Percent S&P 500 Index, 30 Percent Lehman Brothers Government/Corporate Bond Index

□ Competitive Challenges Universe Three-Year CAGR

— Competitive Challenges Universe CAGR Minus Weighted Three-Year CAGR

[a]Compound annual growth rate.

manager has any performance hiccup or if performance firmwide trails off and the firm has very little net new flows, the economics of the firm will be altered, which will affect its bonus pools, investment plans, and so forth. In the next 20 years, the more successful firms will be the ones that have a disproportionate amount of their growth coming from net new flows compared with market appreciation.

Many people believe in the myth that as firms get bigger, they have greater margins because an increasing proportion of every dollar drops to the bottom line. This myth is not supported by the data. Our study finds that no correlation exists between aggregate growth rates and size. Furthermore, if anything, profit margins tend to drop as firms move toward the very large end of the scale ($100 billion and greater in revenue). No correlation exists between profit margin and revenue or between profit margin and assets under management for firms between $1 billion and $100 billion.

Business Archetypes

In our opinion, firms are defined by their competitive focus, not the amount of assets under management. We put every firm in the industry into one of three camps—lifestyle, boutique, or enterprise company—according to its competitive focus.

Lifestyle. Lifestyle firms are dominated by a single individual, tend to be in one segment of the business, and have one product focus. They are usually very profit oriented and are driven by a founder. Many of these firms are in the highest margin category but are not necessarily the fastest growing firms. Nor are they necessarily the best places to work for those who are not the founder or owners. Nevertheless, no evidence exists that these firms will be squeezed out in the next 10 years.

Boutique. Boutique firms have decided that they need broader skill sets than lifestyle firms and that they will participate in more than one segment of the business. They have an internal turf battle going on between the founders and the second-generation managers for control and independence, and they often debate selling. The issue these firms must address is reinvestment versus profits. There is such a thing as being too profitable in this business, which sounds heretical but is absolutely true. Many of the folks in the lifestyle firms have adjusted pretax profit margins of 60–80 percent, much of which is neither redistributed to those who work at the firm nor put back into the firm itself. Generally, the profits are redistributed in boutique and enterprise firms.

Enterprise. Enterprise firms are growth oriented and have multiple products and services. They are customer-solution oriented and reinvest a high proportion of their profits back into the firm. The firms that have made the enterprise bet are not always the largest firms, but they tend to be large because they need revenue to support their extremely broad product and distribution plans. They spend a ton of money on technology, branding, and advertising. These include such firms as Putnam and Citigroup, and some smaller firms ($3 billion to $10 billion in assets) have decided that their futures lie in becoming enterprise firms. The managers of these small enterprise firms are betting that their firms will outlive their own lives as well as the lives of the folks in the lifestyle firms.

Future Direction

At Investment Counseling, we are preoccupied with what it means to be an online and digital competitor in the future, regardless of firm size or market segment. **Exhibit 1** shows a number of online competitors that are providing investment services to some degree. The idea that these online companies are not playing in the same world as traditional investment managers is a joke. Every high-net-worth investment firm and every Registered Investment Adviser (RIA) I have talked to has had some preoccupation or concern about whether these services are in the best interests of their clients, whether they can duplicate some of these services for their clients, or whether they are trash and should be thrown out. In the next 10–20 years, every investment manager will fit somewhere on a grid such as that in Exhibit 1, whether through its Web site or through its ability to deal with clients and transact online.

Meeting of Old and New. The whole world heretofore has been an offline world. The traditional advice providers have been pension consultants, brokers, insurance agents, and so on. The portals have been law firms, banks, insurers, and wirehouses. In the online world, the advice providers are Charles Schwab & Company, E*TRADE Securities, and others who are fighting it out and trying to get through portals such as Yahoo!, Microsoft Corporation, and America Online. The old-line infomediaries, the places or the publications where investors got information (such as the *Wall Street Journal*, *Pensions & Investments*, and CNBC), are now meeting head-on the new choices (such as TheStreet.com, www.Morningstar.com, and InvestorForce.com, formerly PlanSponsorExchange.com). **Figure 2** shows the meeting of the online and offline investment worlds.

Exhibit 1. Online Investment Services Providers

Site/URL	News/Information/Research	Advisory Services	Brokerage	Supermarket	Other Financial Services
CNNfn Interactive www.cnnfn.com	×				
MSN MoneyCentral Investor investor.msn.com	×				
TheStreet.com www.thestreet.com	×				
DirectAdvice.com www.directadvice.com	×	×			
Financial Engines www.financialengines.com	×	×			
FundAlarm www.fundalarm.com	×	×			
Merrill Lynch & Company www.ml.com	×	×	×		×
The Motley Fool www.fool.com	×	×			
E*TRADE Securities www.etrade.com	×	×	×	×	
Charles Schwab & Company www.schwab.com	×	×	×	×	×
Fidelity Investments www.fidelity.com	×	×	×	×	×
The Vanguard Group www.vanguard.com	×	×	×	×	×

Figure 2. Offline and Online Investment Worlds

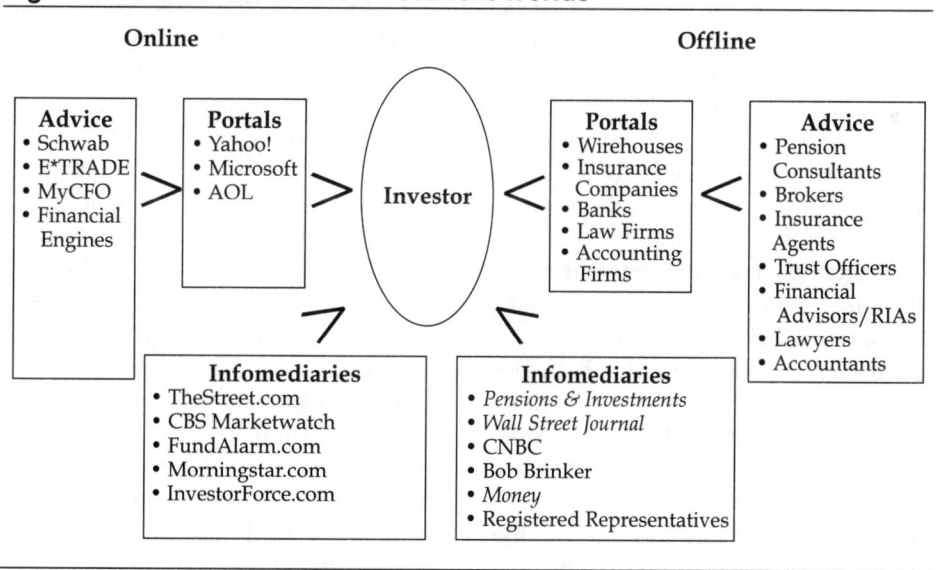

Online

- **Advice**: Schwab, E*TRADE, MyCFO, Financial Engines
- **Portals**: Yahoo!, Microsoft, AOL
- **Infomediaries**: TheStreet.com, CBS Marketwatch, FundAlarm.com, Morningstar.com, InvestorForce.com

Investor

Offline

- **Portals**: Wirehouses, Insurance Companies, Banks, Law Firms, Accounting Firms
- **Advice**: Pension Consultants, Brokers, Insurance Agents, Trust Officers, Financial Advisors/RIAs, Lawyers, Accountants
- **Infomediaries**: *Pensions & Investments*, *Wall Street Journal*, CNBC, Bob Brinker, *Money*, Registered Representatives

Investment managers and RIAs need to think of themselves as portals that marry the online and offline—the conduits through which all client inquiries need to go. If they do not make any changes, many firms will not survive. InvestorForce.com, for example, gives plan sponsors performance attribution, product analysis, and other investment-related information, so plan sponsors can bypass the pension consultant three-quarters of the time. This firm, and others like it, will tremendously lower the impact that pension consultants have on the flow of funds in the future. Pension consultants will have to come up with much more valuable services than they have currently or half of them will go out of business.

Figure 3 illustrates the current interaction of the old investing world (right side) with the new (left side). The new world, as in the old, relies heavily on

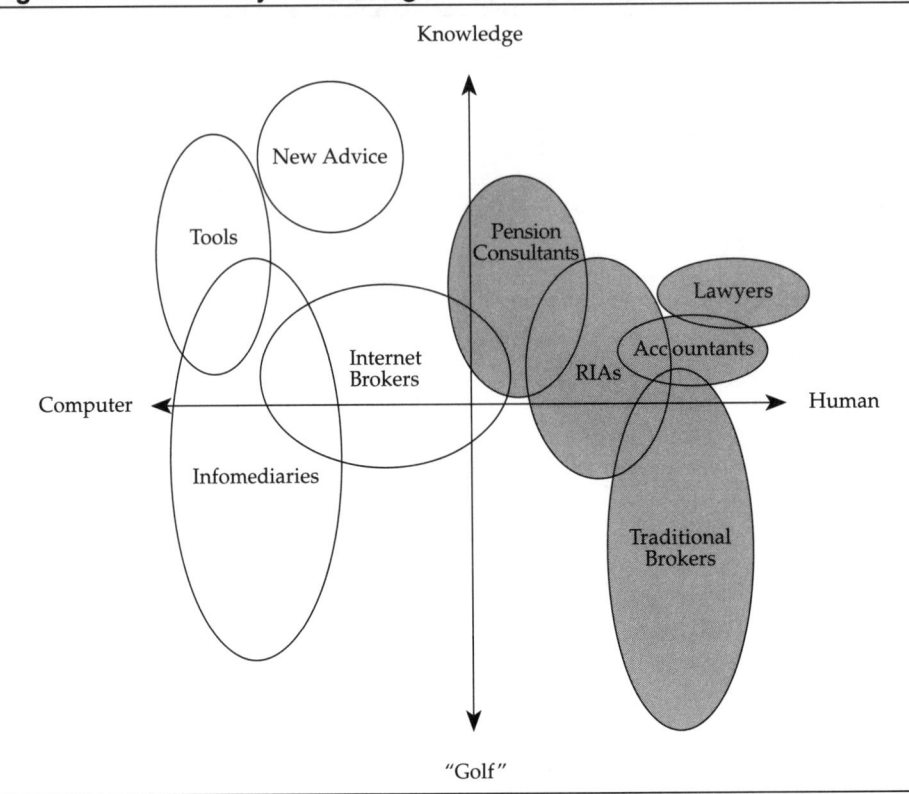

Figure 3. Intermediary Positioning of Old and New World

[Figure 3: A two-axis diagram with vertical axis labeled "Knowledge" (top) and "Golf" (bottom), and horizontal axis from "Computer" (left) to "Human" (right). On the left (computer) side are unshaded ellipses labeled: New Advice, Tools, Internet Brokers, Infomediaries. On the right (human) side are shaded ellipses labeled: Pension Consultants, Lawyers, RIAs, Accountants, Traditional Brokers.]

knowledge, but the new world is far less reliant on "golf-type" relationships (i.e., relationships with an entertainment focus) than the old. The new world consists of new advice providers (such as Financial Engines, DirectAdvice.com, and mPower Advisors, formerly called 401k Forum), Internet brokers, infomediaries (such as TheStreet.com), and tools (such as Intuit's Quicken and Microsoft's Money). Some strong and emerging providers are trying to marry the two worlds. In 10–15 years, many more firms on the right will have chosen to marry their business and services with the applications on the left; those that have not will generally be a small group, few of which will be successful, and they will stay on the right-hand side. As these new entrants come in on the left, they are scaring the traditional intermediaries on the right.

Organizational Structure. In the future, the organizational blueprint of firms will have to change. In the old world, the foundation of a firm is its infrastructure and back-office technology, as **Figure 4** shows. On top of that comes client databases and how a firm brands its efforts, or at least markets its efforts. At the top is selling and managing clients.

In the new world, as **Figure 5** shows, firms will need a technology infrastructure underlying the whole firm. Next will come client database management for the whole firm, followed by brand management (traditional and online) and Web site management. Even a small firm will have one or two people working on this underlying platform because it will be critical to success. Currently, not 10–15 years from now, a lot of people are spending significant money and resources on this underlying platform. All firms—whether institutional, high net worth, or retail—will need this platform, and the people creating and maintaining it will be paid in parity with chief investment officers and investment professionals. Heretofore, these people have been relegated to the back of the office.

On top of this underlying platform will come traditional marketing, client service, and sales, but running in tandem will be customized content and Internet distribution.

To be successful in the future, a firm's Web site must have the following four elements:

- *Community.* Firms will need to establish a sense of community and interactivity. They will need to provide advice, links to other Web sites, account access, and chat rooms.
- *Content.* Firms will need to differentiate themselves from each other by the content they provide on their Web sites. They will need to provide media and news, up-to-date information, and research and reports.
- *Segmentation.* Firms will need to segment their Web sites for the 401(k) market, wealthy individuals, educational purposes, and so on.

Figure 4. Old World Organizational Blueprint

[Diagram showing three parallel columns for Institutional Client, Private Client, and Retail Client. Each column has Sales arrow at top, followed by stacked boxes: Marketing and Client Service, Brand Management, Client Database Management, Technology Infrastructure Management.]

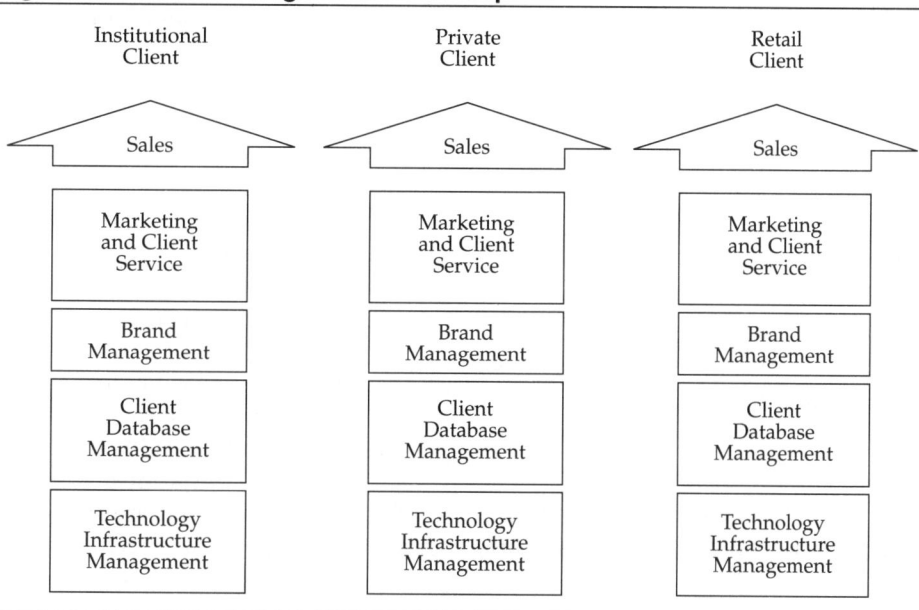

Figure 5. New World Organizational Blueprint

[Diagram showing three columns for Institutional Client, Private Client, and Retail Client. Each column has Traditional Sales and Internet Distribution arrows at top, followed by Marketing and Client Services and Customized Content boxes. Shared horizontal layers across all three columns: Web Site, Brand Management (Traditional and Online), Client Database Management, Technology Infrastructure Management.]

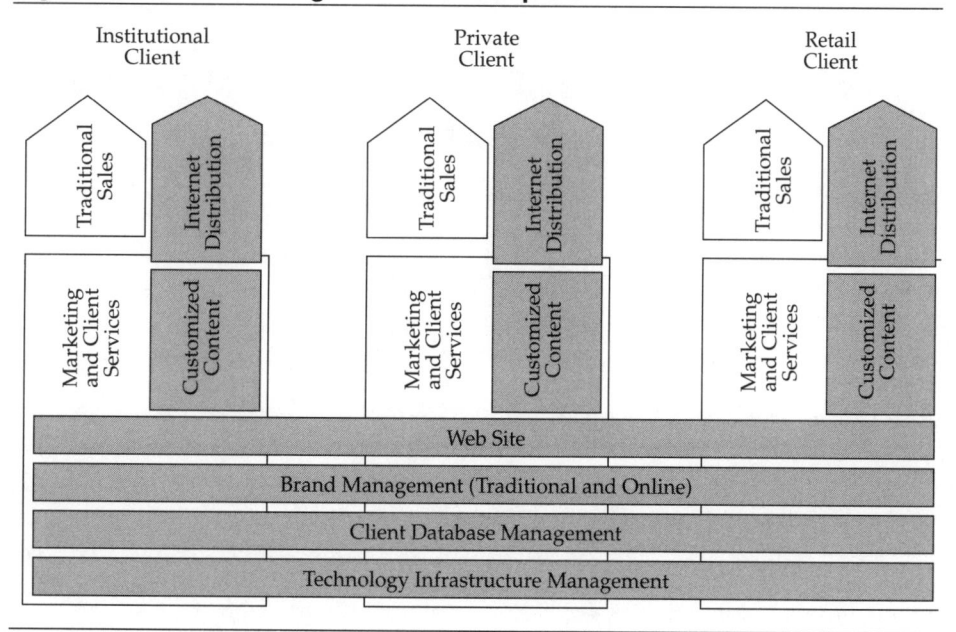

- *Branding.* Branding will take on an added focus. Firms must be able to distinguish their Web sites from those of other firms and create a memorable client experience.

Talent Gap. In the old world, the people who got all the money and who ran the company were the chief investment officers, portfolio managers, high-level salespeople, and maybe directors of operations or chief operating officers. In the future, these people will still be important and will still get a significant share of the compensation pie, but some other people will be sharing the pie with them: chief information officers, Web site strategists, investment product managers, brand managers, media relations managers, client solutions specialists, and knowledge engineers. What most investment firms have missed in the past five years is paying people "what the market pays them." To remain competitive, a firm—whether it is a lifestyle, boutique, or enterprise firm—will have to compensate people according to the standards set by the market, or else it will drive these people away.

Evaluation. Morningstar and Lipper have become the standards in evaluating investment products, and the AIMR-PPS™ standards have set the benchmark for comparing investment performance. Just six or seven years ago, being in compliance with the AIMR-PPS standards was not that common; it has shot up during the past five years. In the next 20 years, we believe that the industry will move toward a business scorecard that evaluates the capability of people to grow their firms wisely, put in the appropriate organizational services and technology platforms, show important employee retention and employee motivation, and a whole set of other factors. Currently, public companies have to provide that kind of information for analysts. In the future, managers will have to give it to clients.

Conclusion

The competitive challenges facing the investment management industry in the future will be both similar to and different from those facing firms today. Client service should remain at the top as a determinant of success, but employee satisfaction should rise in importance and product capability should drop in importance. Firms will also have to find a way to measure productivity if they want to measure their success.

The successful investment firm of the future will have figured out a way to combine its traditional business operations with the functionalities of the Internet; it will have found a way to be a portal between the traditional investment world and the new Internet-focused investment world. Consequently, it will have at its base a technology infrastructure that includes client data management and Web-based services.

Certainly, no one knows exactly what the future will look like. But trends are already under way, and firms that ignore those trends will be left behind.

Question and Answer Session

Charles B. Burkhart, Jr.

Question: What are the most effective ways to assess client wants and needs for the high-net-worth environment?

Burkhart: Firms need to do more in the way of formal assessments. They should have people whose job it is to formally assess and survey clients, and they should do it regularly. Firms should host events that are not boondoggles. They should spend a lot of quality time talking about the client's generational and financial planning issues, even if they don't handle that part of the client's world.

An important question that is not frequently asked is: Who else manages a client's money? At least half the time, firms don't know the answer to that question. They don't know the client's total bucket, and they don't know the parts of the bucket they have. If firms cannot answer such questions, they will lose clients to those firms that can.

Question: Given that client service is so important, what should firms do to excel at client service?

Burkhart: One way to excel at client service is to provide a differentiated client experience. In the current environment of growing market turbulence and increasing customer sophistication, firms need to pay attention to educating clients on issues that are important to the clients and/or pertinent to their portfolios. Given the highly competitive environment in the investment industry, not doing so may have negative consequences. So, standing out from the competition, beyond just performance, is the top job for the next 20 years.

Another way to excel at client service is to evaluate the client experience. As part of our "Competitive Challenges" survey, we ask firms how they survey their clients. Not surprisingly, a lot of people do not do much at all, and what they do do is informal. Generally, retail firms spend the most money and time on client assessment, and they do it the most formally. Private-client and high-net-worth firms give it the least attention. Institutional firms are somewhere in the middle.

The areas that firms should care more about than they do are additional contribution analysis (i.e., how much more of your clients' money do you manage today than when they became your clients?), client tenure analysis (i.e., how long-lived are your clients?), formal feedback from clients, and informal feedback from client service personnel.

Question: What are the challenges to being successful in the future?

Burkhart: One of the biggest problems we encounter is a firm's ability (or should I say inability) to take the knowledge out of the hands of one or two people and make the firm less insular and less parochial by disseminating the knowledge throughout the firm. What happens in most firms is that information about the firm—its clients' preferences, its market data, and its performance issues—tends to go to a few people and stay with those people. Those people either die or leave, and the information never gets passed on to others. In the next 20 years, some people's sole job (investment managers and the intermediaries to those managers) will be to get all this knowledge and make sure that it gets disseminated appropriately and resides with a broad base of people at the firm.

At this point, some of the best knowledge providers are Vanguard for client education, Schwab for knowledge packaging, Amazon.com for customization, and Capital One Financial Corporation (the credit card and bank-like firm) for data mining. Capital One knows more about how to mine data from a customer than any other firm I have seen, which is a skill that is sorely lacking in the money management business. Compared with Capital One and Amazon, investment managers know little about their customers. That situation will change greatly, and firms will have to pay serious money to maintain people to do such analysis.

Selected Publications

AIMR

AIMR Performance Presentation Standards Handbook, 2nd edition, 1997
Alternative Investing, 1998
Asian Equity Investing, 1998
Asset Allocation in a Changing World, 1998
Credit Analysis Around the World, 1998
Currency Risk in Investment Portfolios, 1999
Derivatives in Portfolio Management, 1998
Equity Research and Valuation Techniques, 1998
Frontiers in Credit-Risk Analysis, 1999
The Future of Investment Management, 1998
Investment Counseling for Private Clients, 1999
Practical Issues in Equity Analysis, 2000
Risk Management: Principles and Practices, 1999
Standards of Practice Handbook, 8th ed., 1999
The Technology Industry: Impact of the Internet, 2000

Research Foundation

Company Performance and Measures of Value Added, 1996
by Pamela P. Peterson, CFA, and David R. Peterson

Controlling Misfit Risk in Multiple-Manager Investment Programs, 1998
by Jeffery V. Bailey, CFA, and David E. Tierney

Country Risk in Global Financial Management, 1997
by Claude B. Erb, CFA, Campbell R. Harvey, and Tadas E. Viskanta

Economic Foundations of Capital Market Returns, 1997
by Brian D. Singer, CFA, and Kevin Terhaar, CFA

Interest Rate Modeling and the Risk Premiums in Interest Rate Swaps, 1997
by Robert Brooks, CFA

The International Equity Commitment, 1998
by Stephen A. Gorman

Investment Styles, Market Anomalies, and Global Stock Selection, 1999
by Richard O. Michaud

Long-Range Forecasting, 1999
by William S. Gray, CFA

Sales-Driven Franchise Value, 1997
by Martin L. Leibowitz

The Welfare Effects of Soft Dollar Brokerage: Law and Economics, 2000
by Stephen M. Horan, CFA, and D. Bruce Johnsen